## WHAT PEOPLE ARE SAYING ABOUT
# QBQ! AND Parenting the QBQ Way

"*QBQ!* is the best book on personal responsibility and accountability available and is required reading for my team!"

—Dave Ramsey, host of *The Dave Ramsey Show* and author of
*Total Money Makeover* and *EntreLeadership*

"*Parenting the QBQ Way* is written with and from the heart of parents who have been through the joys, triumphs, and challenges that all moms and dads face. Thanks to John and Karen Miller for this great tool to add to our parenting toolbox!"

—Angie Mozilo, mother of three and host of *Mom of Many Hats*

"John and Karen Miller have hit it out of the park! This book is full of practical approaches and keen insights for better parenting. The ideas are thought-provoking, funny, and easy to implement. This is a must-read for every parent. Grandparents, too!"

—Jim Loscheider, father of four, grandfather of four, and
Vice President of Donor Ministries, Samaritan's Purse

"I couldn't put *Parenting the QBQ Way* down! I can't say I've ever finished another book on parenting. They are too long, complicated, and boring. But not this book! Simple, logical, and fun to read—and fabulous for parents with children of any age."

—Kristin Smart, mother of two and
human resources manager of Schwan's Foods

"The Millers teach us the critical nature of personal accountability in parenting. Whether you are thinking of having kids, have toddlers crawling about, or your children have left the nest, I cannot recommend this book highly enough!"

—Brad Meuli, father of three, grandfather of three, and
CEO of Denver Rescue Mission

*continued . . .*

"Absolutely the best book on parenting I've ever read. I'm buying copies for each of my grown children—today!"

—Susie Sharkey, mother of three, grandmother of six, and
retired first grade teacher

"Right on target! I love the wide variety of wisdom, as well as John and Karen's easy-to-read writing. The content is outstanding!"

—Mark Hardacre, father of three and
pastor of Crossroads Community Church

"*Parenting the QBQ Way* is a breath of fresh air to the parent who has been overwhelmed with various parenting methods. It has changed the way I parent. The Millers teach a new way of thinking without giving overwhelmed parents another to-do list!"

—Katelin Bjerkaas, stay-at-home mother of two

"The best way to raise an accountable generation is to ensure that we, as parents, make personal accountability a core value in the home. *Parenting the QBQ Way* is the tool to do just that."

—Kevin Brown, father of one and assistant vice president of ServPro

"I can't say enough for this commonsense and loving method of helping children become adults. In such a chaotic world, this book gives hope to parents. I've recommended this book to my grandchildren who are now having children! I wish I'd had a resource so down-to-earth when I was a young mother. Dr. Spock didn't have a clue!"

—Judy McCormick, mother of four, grandmother of twelve,
and great-grandmother of two

"I have used the *QBQ!* book in my business for years! Now, my wife and I are applying QBQ concepts to the raising of our children, and we've been amazed at the positive outcome at home."

—Steve Jones, father of three and president of Tenacity Investment Group

# Parenting the QBQ Way

[Expanded Edition]

## HOW TO BE AN OUTSTANDING PARENT AND RAISE GREAT KIDS USING THE POWER OF PERSONAL ACCOUNTABILITY

**JOHN G. MILLER**

with Karen G. Miller

A Perigee Book

**A PERIGEE BOOK**
**Published by the Penguin Group**
**Penguin Group (USA) Inc.**
**375 Hudson Street, New York, New York 10014, USA**

Penguin Group (Canada), 90 Eglinton Avenue East, Suite 700, Toronto, Ontario M4P 2Y3, Canada (a division of Pearson Penguin Canada Inc.) • Penguin Books Ltd., 80 Strand, London WC2R 0RL, England • Penguin Ireland, 25 St. Stephen's Green, Dublin 2, Ireland (a division of Penguin Books Ltd.) • Penguin Group (Australia), 707 Collins Street, Melbourne, Victoria 3008, Australia (a division of Pearson Australia Group Pty Ltd.) • Penguin Books India Pvt. Ltd., 11 Community Centre, Panchsheel Park, New Delhi—110 017, India • Penguin Group (NZ), 67 Apollo Drive, Rosedale, Auckland 0632, New Zealand (a division of Pearson New Zealand Ltd.) • Penguin Books, Rosebank Office Park, 181 Jan Smuts Avenue, Parktown North 2193, South Africa • Penguin China, B7 Jaiming Center, 27 East Third Ring Road North, Chaoyang District, Beijing 100020, China

Penguin Books Ltd., Registered Offices: 80 Strand, London WC2R 0RL, England

PUBLISHING HISTORY
G. P. Putnam's Sons electronic edition / March 2012
Perigee trade paperback expanded edition / December 2012

Library of Congress Cataloging-in-Publication Data

Miller, John G, 1958–
Parenting the QBQ way : how to be an outstanding parent and raise great kids using the power of personal accountability / John G. Miller with Karen G. Miller.
p.  cm.
"A Perigee book."
ISBN 978-0-399-16192-6
1. Parenting.  2. Child rearing.  3. Responsibility.  4. Choice (Psychology)  5. Decision making.  6. Problem solving.  I. Miller, Karen G.  II. Title.
HQ755.8.M55  2013
306.874—dc23          2012032252

PRINTED IN THE UNITED STATES OF AMERICA

10  9  8  7  6  5  4  3  2  1

Most Perigee books are available at special quantity discounts for bulk purchases for sales promotions, premiums, fund-raising, or educational use. Special books, or book excerpts, can also be created to fit specific needs. For details, write: Special Markets, Penguin Group (USA) Inc., 375 Hudson Street, New York, New York 10014.

# · Contents ·

# · Contents ·

# · Foreword ·

*Conspicuously absent from the Ten Commandments
is any obligation of parent to child. We must suppose
that God felt it unnecessary to command by law
what He had ensured by love.*

—ROBERT BRAULT

My parents, John and Karen Miller, are not parenting experts—but I believe they are expert parents. While they do not have degrees in child psychology and have not performed research studies or pursued PhDs in family counseling, their accomplishments as parents are evident. As the oldest of their children, I think I can make this claim: They may not be perfect, but they are awfully good at this job they chose.

I know that I sound like a child boasting about her parents, but I'm not only the oldest of seven—six girls and one boy—I am on the QBQ Inc. team helping my dad spread the message of *personal accountability* through training, speaking, and coaching. And in spite of what many believe is a very hard thing to do—work in a family business—I *love* working for and with my parents. That alone might tell you something about their effectiveness in parenting.

Sure, they've made their mistakes and I've made mine, but all in all, I've had a great relationship with them through the years, and still do. I remember being fairly baffled at some of my friends' struggles with their parents. While I certainly had some "non-harmonious" moments with mine, I never wanted out or wished they'd go away.

One of the core reasons I believe they are good parents is they employ a practical and powerful idea called "The Question Behind the Question," a tool that enables them—or any mom and dad—to practice personal accountability in parenting. And if parents could have only one tool in their parenting toolbox, it should definitely be the QBQ.

My dad first created the QBQ before I was a teenager. He then began teaching his message of "Personal Accountability and the QBQ" to the corporate world. Early on, he discovered that clients wanted to use the material at home to become outstanding moms and dads. He frequently heard people say, "I can use this as much with my family as I can on the job!"

The language of the QBQ soon began seeping into the everyday conversations of families, including the Miller household. My siblings and I sometimes tease our parents, especially my father, with, "Um, Dad, do *you* need to ask a QBQ right now?!" Of course, it's all in fun but I really can say we are a QBQ family.

The good news is any family can become one.

I believe that parents are hungry for tools to help them in the raising of their kids. Parenting is a tough 24/7 job. I've always suspected that, but now I *know* it since becoming a mom myself. My husband, Erik, and I are grateful for this practical tool called the QBQ, and I know other parents are, too. I receive emails from parents who share their parenting struggles and how they're applying QBQ at home to do a better job raising their children.

But the reality is, the original *QBQ! The Question Behind the Question* book was not specifically written with parents in mind. I remember one grandmother who heard my father on *The Dave Ramsey Radio Show* and immediately bought *QBQ!* and *Flipping the Switch* from our website. Soon after, she asked if she could return them. When asked why, she said they were "all about business" and she had wanted the books for her adult kids to read and use in their raising of her grandchildren.

Over lunch one day, I was talking with a friend who has two young ones. As we chatted about our lives as moms, she told me, "The last thing I want is another step-by-step parenting book that tells me *exactly* what I'm supposed to do. So much of that kind of content doesn't seem to apply. What I need are ideas that challenge me, and principles that can guide me to do my parenting job better." I responded simply, "My parents are writing a book for you."

So, here is *Parenting the QBQ Way*—written for parents, grandparents, and anyone else interested in discovering terrific ways to raise great children. We believe there is a real need for this content for this reason: Parenting is a *learned* skill. With that in mind, I promise that you will discover practical and powerful ideas that—through your commitment to putting them into action—will become skills over time. In this there will be many rewards!

—Kristin E. Lindeen
Kristin@QBQ.com
www.QBQ.com

# Parenting the QBQ Way

# CHAPTER ONE

# Personal Accountability

*You cannot escape the responsibility of
tomorrow by evading it today.*
—ABRAHAM LINCOLN

Our twentysomething daughter Molly was in charge of a neighbor's twelve-year-old boy for a weekend while his parents traveled. On Saturday morning, Molly brought him over to hang out at our house, along with his buddy Grayson. We'd never met Grayson, nor had we met Grayson's mom and dad. We don't know what they're like, where they're from, or what they do for a living, but we do know *something* about them. They left clear evidence—in Grayson.

We live on a couple acres of Colorado land with a big barn and a swimming pool. There are signs everywhere that this has been home to seven children: a trampoline, a rope to swing on, a well-worn four-wheeler, and lots of indoor "techno toys." It's a place our kids—Kristin, Tara, Michael, Molly, Charlene, Jazzy, and Natasha—have truly enjoyed.

So for many hours the boys had tons of fun and the day flew by.

Around 7 p.m., Molly yelled, "Guys, time to go!" Hearing high-energy footsteps and the swift opening and closing of doors, we assumed they'd all left the house, so we were startled when Grayson appeared in our living room.

"Thanks for letting me come over, Mr. and Mrs. Miller!"

"You're welcome," we replied. "Hope you had fun."

"I sure did!"

"Come again, okay?" Karen said.

"I will. Thanks!"

"Terrific! See ya, Grayson."

"Okay. Have a good evening. Bye!"

*Hmm, did we just interact with an engaging young person who demonstrated courtesy and gratitude? Did he actually say, "Have a good evening"?*

And instantly we knew this: He didn't pick any of that up by watching television. He learned it from his mom and dad because, like children everywhere, he is a product of his parents' parenting.

Some people will pursue the "nature versus nurture" debate, but we'd rather not go there in this book. Sure, some traits or characteristics might be born into our kids, but the danger in thinking about the impact of "nature" is that we'll use nature as an excuse for whatever our children are like if we're not careful. Since this book is focused on *personal accountability* in parenting, we prefer to encourage all dads and moms—including ourselves—to look beyond how we parent for reasons why our children think, feel, or act the way they do. Today many people talk about "character building" for children and that's important, but the truth is, the character of a child is rooted in the way he or she is raised.

We know that this is a difficult notion for some parents to accept, so we're going to say it early to set a tone of personal accountability:

**If parents have problems with their teen, they likely had problems with their toddler.**

Recently, a parent shared this with us:

Our eighth-grade son is driving us crazy! Each week he's supposed to empty all of the trash cans in the house, consolidate the garbage into *bags*—not cans— and place them by the curb for pickup. But he routinely places one of our large cans on the street instead, knowing it's the wrong way to do it! And this isn't the only area we see this sort of behavior. When he doesn't set his alarm at night and oversleeps, he blames his sister for not getting him up. If we tell him to stop playing games on the computer and do his homework instead, he initially ignores us and then says we're "mean." When he doesn't practice his piano lesson, he takes absolutely no accountability for his lack of preparedness for the next time he's with his teacher. What do we do? *Help!*

This is an awfully frustrating situation—and we truly feel for these parents—but problems like these don't appear overnight. They are a result of the parents' practices through the child's lifetime. So the wrong questions to ask are "Why is my child so difficult?" and "When will he change?" (We refer to these kinds of questions as Incorrect Questions, or IQs.) The right questions would be "What have *I* done to create my current problems?" and "How can *I* start parenting differently?" Questions like these, which we call QBQs, not only represent accountable thinking but also lead to learning—and where there is learning there is change. For many parents, one key change needed is the willingness to adopt this principle:

**My child is a product of my parenting.**

We know that some will want to debate this, pointing to other influences in a child's life. It's understandable. But we've found it's easier to practice personal accountability in our parenting by not fighting this principle and instead embracing it. With this premise in place, regardless of the age of the child, any parent can become the outstanding mom or dad they wish to be.

# CHAPTER TWO

# Parenting Is a Learned Skill

*Before I got married, I had six theories about bringing up*
*children; now I have six children, and no theories.*

—JOHN WILMOT

**K**aren settled into her seat for a two-hour flight. Directly behind her sat an adorable little boy, about four years old, flanked by his parents. Like most normal little guys, he was pretty active. Karen knew this because he was kicking her seat nonstop and they hadn't even lifted off!

This continued for several minutes until the dad threatened his son:

"If you keep kicking the lady's seat, Santa won't bring you anything for Christmas."

Overhearing the father's statement, Karen felt bad for the child. She was tempted to turn around to say, "It's okay. No problem!" but before she could, the behavior worsened—not the child's but the *parents'* behavior! The mom chimed in with this menacing message: "If you don't stop now, the police will come and take you to jail."

After the flight got under way, the little tyke settled down with a coloring book. All was peaceful, until the mom admonished, "You're coloring too hard. You're going to break the crayons. And stay inside the lines!"

About twenty minutes later the boy was given a DVD player with no headphones and allowed to loudly broadcast a movie for the next hour, disrupting the conversations, thoughts, and sleep of passengers all around him!

When the flight ended and the deplaning process began, Karen heard the couple say this: "Now I know why my parents gave us a shot of brandy before we traveled. Maybe we should try that next time!"

We all know that flying with small children can be challenging, but certainly we can all agree that the parents in this story could have handled their young son in a more effective manner. There is no doubt that they could benefit from a few parenting tips—but what mom or dad can't improve? As Kristin noted in the foreword, parenting is a *learned* skill. When moms and dads just "wing it" and don't seek any training to be the best parents they can be, the results they get may not be the results they hoped for when they chose the job. The truth is, we can all absorb new ideas, implement new practices, and form new habits—and when we do, both the parent and the child win.

# CHAPTER THREE

# QBQ! The Question Behind the Question

*A prudent question is one half of wisdom.*

—FRANCIS BACON

Personal accountability is a powerful principle that can help any mom or dad eliminate victim thinking, complaining, procrastination, and blame from their parenting. When we lament about what our children are doing or not doing, when we delay action while waiting for others to "do something," when we point fingers looking for "whodunit"—we are not putting personal accountability into action.

But we can, and we do it through a tool called the QBQ.

QBQ stands for "The Question Behind the Question," and here's how it is defined:

**QBQ is a tool that enables parents to practice personal accountability by making better choices in the moment.**

And we accomplish this by asking better questions of ourselves. When faced with a parenting problem or frustration, our minds first tend to fill with questions like "Why won't my kids listen?" and "When will they do what I ask?" These questions are natural and understandable, but by focusing on everything and everyone *except* the person asking them, they demonstrate a lack of personal accountability. It's only when we stop and look *behind* those first questions that we find better ones—QBQs—like "What can I do differently?" and "How can I improve as a parent?" Asking *these* questions turns the focus back on ourselves and to what we can do to make a difference. It's nearly impossible to overstate the positive impact this simple change can have on our lives—and on our families.

The QBQ is a practical parenting tool that has three easy-to-apply guidelines to show us how to construct *accountable* questions:

1. QBQs begin with the words "What" or "How"—not "Why," "When," or "Who."
   a. "Why?" questions lead to victim thinking and complaining, as in "Why is parenting so hard?" or "Why isn't my child a better student?"
   b. "When?" questions lead to procrastination, as in "When will my kids start doing what I ask?" or "When will someone take care of that problem?"

    c. "Who?" questions lead to blame and finger-pointing, as in "Who did it?" or "Who's going to help my child get better grades?"

2. QBQs contain the personal pronoun "I"—not "they," "you," or even "we"—because I can change only me. Example: "What can I do?"

3. QBQs always focus on action. Personal accountability is all about engaging in positive behavior now, making it possible for us to contribute and make a difference.

The underlying concept of the QBQ is this:

**The answers are in the questions.**

When we ask better questions, we get better answers. The QBQ guidelines show us how to build—and ask—better questions. We'll also explore the types of questions to avoid asking, but first here's a key point: QBQs are questions we generally ask of *ourselves.* The QBQ is a tool designed to help us reframe our *own* thinking. Certainly, there are some QBQs we can speak out loud—such as "What can I do to serve you?"—but more often than not a QBQ is a better question that we each ask of ourselves, because it's all about *us* discovering those better answers.

Furthermore, just as the QBQ helps us ask better questions, it guides us in making *better choices.* Parents have countless opportunities each day to make choices. And what is it that we are always choosing? *Our next thought.* A compelling opportunity for change exists in these individual moments when we can change our thinking. By helping us make better choices, the QBQ enables us to take charge of our thoughts and literally transform our lives—and our parenting.

We know that moms and dads are looking for practical tools, and it's our belief that the QBQ *is* the how-to needed to parent more effectively. And to learn how to apply the QBQ, we must have some language and structure. "Incorrect Questions" (IQs) are the "Why?," "When?," and "Who?" questions that lead to victim thinking, complaining, procrastination, and blame. If you compare IQs with QBQs, you'll see how simple it can be to put the QBQ into action:

| IQ | QBQ |
| --- | --- |
| *Why doesn't my daughter ever take my advice?* | What can *I* do to understand her needs? |
| *When will my son open up to me?* | How can *I* build a more trusting relationship? |
| *Who made the mess in here?* | What can *I* do to help my child learn good habits? |

Take a moment to review the IQ/QBQ comparisons above. Be aware of how it *feels* to ask an accountable question, a QBQ. Imagine the difference bringing more *personal accountability* to our parenting will make in our families. And rest assured, employing QBQs is a practice one can engage in immediately!

Cory, a thirtysomething salesperson and father of two boys, attended a corporate QBQ training session. Recognizing the value of the QBQ beyond the workplace, he was excited to try it with his family. With the notion of IQs and QBQs fresh in his mind, he pulled his sons to his side and asked, "Boys, what can I do to be a better dad for you?"

He reported that the seven-year-old gave him a hug and the twelve-year-old *gave him a list*!

When we ask accountable questions at home, the answers just might surprise us! But we'll be parenting the QBQ way—and when we do that, everything is better.

# CHAPTER FOUR

# "Why Me?"

*Self-pity is our worst enemy, and if we yield to it,*
*we can never do anything wise in this world.*

—HELEN KELLER

As we begin our journey of using the QBQ to become better parents, keep this thought in mind: The victim parent is a whiny parent. And who wants to be around a whiner?

Victim thinking in parenting starts with asking Incorrect Questions (IQs) like:

"Why don't I get more help around here?"
"Why doesn't my toddler just eat what I feed her?"
"Why won't my children obey me?"
"Why aren't the teachers more supportive?"
"Why won't my daughter work harder?"
"Why isn't my son more responsible?"
"Why is this so difficult?"

Parenting is difficult, but these "poor me" questions take parents straight to the classic pity party. With all due respect, we believe dads and moms who ask "Why me?" questions might need to be put in "time-out"!

Sheri, the mother of an eleven-year-old and a full-time employee at a pharmaceutical firm, emailed us expressing frustration over her relationship with her daughter, Amy. Post-divorce, Sheri was raising a tween all by herself and felt that she was often too tense, yelling too much, and simply not handling single parenting well. But she didn't know how to do it differently. Admittedly, there had been many ineffective "Why?" IQs asked:

"Why don't you study harder?"
"Why are you so moody all the time?"
"Why won't you clean your room like I ask?"
"Why can't you hang out with different kids?"

Then Sheri went through "Personal Accountability and the QBQ!" training at work. As Sheri and her colleagues learned how to ask QBQs on the job, a lightbulb went off in her head. It occurred to her that she could be asking better questions *at home.*

That evening, she asked her daughter this QBQ:

"How can I be a better mom for you right now?"

The floodgates opened. Before Sheri knew it, Amy blurted out, "You could stop dissing my friends all the time!" Sheri was stunned. Of all the stuff she thought might come out, she didn't expect this. Thoughts like *Have I been critical of my daughter's friends? Am I a negative mom?* went through her mind. So she calmly responded, "What do you mean, honey? Tell me more."

More than an hour later, Sheri recalled, they finished the most meaningful conversation they'd ever had. Crying and laughing together, a bond was formed, a breakthrough had taken place. Positive memories had been created. All because a parent, who was tempted to fall into the trap of victim thinking by asking dangerous "Why me?" questions, had paused and asked her daughter a question that began with "What" or "How," contained an "I," and focused on action.

Sheri chose the better path of personal accountability simply by replacing IQs such as "Why won't my child change?" and "Why is my kid so rebellious?" with QBQs like "What can *I* do understand her world?," "How can *I* be more effective at home?," and, of course, "What can *I* do to be a better mom for you?"

"The Question Behind the Question" is a wonderfully practical tool that helps us become outstanding parents. And that surely beats victim thinking, because when we play the victim, we serve no one.

# CHAPTER FIVE

# Learn to Earn

*Opportunity is missed by most people because it is
dressed in overalls and looks like work.*

—THOMAS EDISON

Do you agree or disagree with the following statements?

Everyone on an athletic team should receive a
trophy.
Children must have the newest version of all things
electronic.
Thirteen-year-olds deserve limos for their birthday
parties.
Cell phones are not a privilege, they are a right.
Driving is not a privilege, it is a right.

After reading the above we suspect most moms and dads
would respond with "None of them are true!" or "I don't
agree at all!" But the questions accountable parents ask themselves are "Am *I* instilling thoughts and beliefs like these

into *my* child?" and "Have *I* created children who suffer from the dangerous disease of *entitlement thinking*?"

And, of course, this tough-on-self question: "In what ways have *I* become entitled?"

In John's book *Outstanding!*, he asserts that individuals in exceptional organizations put their nose to the grindstone, invest tons of effort and energy, demonstrate a high level of commitment, and get stuff done. In other words, they work—and they work hard. In these organizations, there is little to no entitlement thinking because managers and employees alike believe they must *earn* their pay, *earn* their benefits, and *earn* their rewards. In fact, they *want* to earn these things. Individuals like this know that becoming entitled and possessing an "I deserve!" mentality is not a healthy way to live life.

Honestly, when we experience feelings of entitlement—essentially just another way of playing the victim—are we contributing to the world around us? Are we making a positive difference in the lives of others? Are we adding value to society? Are we learning, growing, and changing while fulfilling our God-given potential?

We suggest the answer to each of these questions is a resounding *No!*

The good news is there is an antidote to the entitlement problem for people of any age, and it's this:

**Learn to earn.**

The challenge, though, for most of us with learning to earn is we live in a world that presents messages of entitlement thinking at every turn. It can be very difficult to protect our families from this unaccountable way of living. But QBQ parents don't complain about "the world," dwelling on the broad political and societal causes of this phenomenon. They work on their *own* entitlement thinking while focusing on how to best parent their kids to prevent them from growing up to be entitled adults.

In this day and age, ensuring that the future workers of the world—our children—live a life of personal accountability requires parental vigilance and hard work, but it's worth it. Along with feelings of accomplishment and satisfaction, people of all ages experience great joy when entitlement and victim thinking are defeated. When we raise our kids to refrain from stretching their hand out asking the world to give them what "they deserve," and instead we give them a hand up by teaching them to learn to earn, we have surely taken a giant step toward raising great kids.

So, since we can't change society but can change ourselves, let's focus on what *we* control. First, we must make certain that we are not thinking unproductive thoughts like *The world owes me* and *I deserve*. If we are, then we are setting the wrong example for our kids. Then, we must parent daily with the goal of creating non-entitled children who want to earn their rewards in life.

Later in this book, we will explore valuable lessons to teach to our kids about money, as we know the topic of money management for children is an important aspect of learning to earn. But as always, when it comes to our core message of personal accountability, everything begins with Dad and Mom asking QBQs like these:

"What can I do to identify and eliminate my own entitlement thinking?"

"How can I demonstrate a solid work ethic for my children?"

"What can I do today to teach my kids the importance of learning to earn?"

# Chapter Six

# No Complaining

*Do everything without grumbling or arguing.*

—PHILIPPIANS 2:14 NIV

The reason we do our best to use the QBQ and now share it with other parents is that we've learned that *we* need it ourselves. We'll give you an example of what we mean.

If you ask Karen whether John ever slips into victim thinking and whining by asking "Why?" questions, she'll tell you that he wears a sign around his neck at home that screams "CHIEF COMPLAINER"! Being a verbal guy, one who likes to express just about every thought he has in the form of declaratory statements, candid observations, and unsolicited counsel, John often sounds like he's complaining. And sometimes he is.

The problem with complaining is, well, everything. It wastes energy and time, while bringing down the "mood" of the home. It rarely adds value. Sure, once in a while complaining can initiate problem solving and something might be made better as a result. Generally, though, complaining is just more victim thinking in the form of a lousy verbal habit that grates on others. Knowing his propensity to complain and the impact it has on the family, John sometimes asks this fairly odd QBQ:

"What can I do right now to keep my big mouth shut?!"

Of course, the better QBQs would be:

"How can I be more positive?"
"What can I do to find the good?"
"How can I offer a solution to the problem?"

Those are outstanding questions and anyone can choose to ask them . . . even kids.

All children complain at some point about their friends, teachers, homework, chores—and being sent outside when they'd rather stare at the TV or computer. But what makes us chuckle are *parents* who complain about their children's complaining! Aren't we now the complainers when we ask, "Why does my child complain so much?" That's definitely an Incorrect Question.

We suggest that it's a parent's job, through gentle, loving confrontation, to teach kids that complaining and whining are totally unproductive. A wise person once said, "My hands are too full to carry a complaint." A good lesson for all of us, especially parents who might be complainers themselves.

Parental accountability is about looking into that proverbial mirror and pondering *Did my child get the habit of complaining from . . . me?* Ben Franklin wrote, "That which hurts also instructs." So as dads and moms, let's engage in some instructive self-reflection—and then ask this QBQ:

"What can I do to be a good example for my child?"

# CHAPTER SEVEN

# Procrastination: The Friend of Failure

*God has promised forgiveness to your repentance, but*
*He has not promised tomorrow to your procrastination.*

—SAINT AUGUSTINE

In John's family home, his mom hung a circular wooden plaque on the kitchen wall with these four letters etched on it: "TUIT." She knew that humans have a natural propensity to say, "I'll get round *to it*," so she simply put a *round* "TUIT" on the wall as a reminder to everyone of how easy it is to put stuff off. She didn't know about the QBQ, but the goal was the same: Take action *now*!

Maybe "getting round to it" is fine when it comes to fixing that old shed lock, mopping the kitchen floor, or picking up the dry cleaning, but it can cost us and our kids dearly when it comes to parenting. Just as we would not lay a foundation for a house, see and ignore obvious cracks, and build anyway—we don't want to be the mom or dad who someday says with regret, "I should've dealt with that a long time ago." Procrastinating parents fall into the "I'll do it later!" trap. They see a problem with their kids that they know they should deal with, but they don't—and the problem just gets worse.

Most of us would not get up in the morning and say, "Today I plan to defer all action to a future time so as to add no value to the life of my child and the well-being of my family!" But when moms and dads ask questions that sound and feel like "When will someone handle this?"—isn't it the same thing? Have you ever heard—or asked—these Incorrect Questions?

> "When will he stop ruling this house with his tantrums?"
> "When will my kids stop fighting so much with each other?"
> "When is my daughter going to speak more respectfully to me?"
> "When will she stop dressing like that?"
> "When is my son going to learn to make good choices?"
> "When is someone going to talk to him about that?"
> "When will they do their chores without being asked?"

Incorrect Questions like these lead us straight to the friend of failure: procrastination. It's best to ask QBQs. Again, QBQs begin with "What" or "How," contain an "I," and focus on *action*. Right now, any QBQ parent can ask, "What action can I take today to make a difference?" and "How can I handle this problem right now?"

# CHAPTER EIGHT

# The Urgency of Now

*I have been impressed with the urgency of doing.*
*Knowing is not enough; we must apply. Being willing*
*is not enough; we must do.*

—LEONARDO DA VINCI

It was 1994 and we were living in Minneapolis. One day during rush hour, Karen was driving westbound on a four-lane highway with the four children we had at the time when her large conversion van—affectionately called "The Mother Ship"—began to stall. She quickly pulled the monster to the left and stopped, facing west, in a position where the vehicle was hugging the center guardrail. Traffic continued to fly by in the two westbound lanes on the right. Trapped and without a cell phone, Karen and her brood found some paper and markers and quickly made a "HELP!!!" sign. Affixing it to the rear window, they settled in to wait.

But then something very unsettling happened. For reasons we'll never know, six-year-old Michael, sitting in the second-row bucket seat on the right, suddenly opened the van door, swinging it directly into the speeding traffic passing by.

When Karen saw what Michael had done, *she took no action*. She just sat there, and then asked herself:

"When will he stop doing those things?"
"When will Michael learn?"
"When will he close the door?"
"When will someone handle this situation?"
"When will I get a little help here?"

Do you believe that? Do you really believe that when immediate action is called for, a parent would sit back and ask lousy questions while risking her child's life? No, of course you don't.

Here's what really happened: Karen lunged from her seat and latched onto Michael's little left forearm, yanking him straight back into the van. The door closed with his hand still on the handle. The cost? A slightly sore shoulder for a six-year-old boy who is still around today to be reminded of a story he barely remembers.

Parents, *now* is almost always better than later.

# CHAPTER NINE

# "Whodunit?"

*It is more difficult to praise rightly than to blame.*
—THOMAS FULLER

Parents are owners. Children are renters.

We were considering buying a house that we could rent to others, but everyone we knew dissuaded us, saying, "Oh, you don't want to be a landlord. Renters don't care about the property and will cause you a lot of headaches!"

So we didn't do it. But we sort of did anyway by having seven kids! It's true: Dads and moms almost always care more about the appearance, cleanliness, and condition of their home than the children do—or ever will. This is no reflection on kids; it's just the way it is. In many ways, children are just "passing through." Because of this "owner versus renter" phenomenon, parents find it easy to ask IQs like:

"Who left the dirty dishes in the sink?"
"Who made the mess in the family room?"

"Who left the wet towels on the bathroom floor?"

"Who tracked mud in all over the hallway floor?"

Would you agree that "owners" find it awfully easy to ask these questions of "renters"? We know we do. The problem is they represent little more than blame and finger-pointing. Questions like these put us right into the blame game because most "Whodunit?" questions are all about finding a culprit and not about solving a problem.

To be sure, parents who seek to become QBQ parents will look at the IQs above and think, *Well, how else do I find out who did this or that?* We understand this dilemma and accept the fact that a "Who?" question must be asked now and then. The question "Who left the socks on the stairs?" is inherently benign—when the *tone* and *intent* are right. However, if the tone is angry, sarcastic, or sharp—and maybe even scary to others—then it is probably an Incorrect Question. Or if the intention is to find the guilty party for the sole purpose of punishment rather than teaching and developing, then the question is definitely an IQ.

If your child leaves socks on the stairs repeatedly when asked not to, then QBQs like these will serve you well: "How can I be more clear about my expectations?" and "What can I do to lay out the consequences that will follow?" As well, QBQs such as "What can I do right now to control my emotions?" and "How can I be the kind of parent I want to be?"

will allow us to be a better mom or dad in that moment when we're frustrated over those stupid socks lying on the stairs!

Simply put, blame and finger-pointing serve no purpose. Be careful not to ask "Whodunit?" questions. Let's discipline ourselves to ask accountable questions that begin with "What" and "How." It'll feel better and we'll scare fewer people.

## · Chapter Ten ·

# No Excuses

*Blame is just a lazy person's way of making sense of chaos.*
—DOUG COUPLAND

Do your kids have characteristics you don't like? If so, where did they get them?

If you're a smart-aleck dad, you're thinking, *Their mom!* And if you're a mother, we know what you're thinking right now.

But beyond thinking playfully (or seriously!) that the fault lies with the other parent, many parents truly do find external reasons—or excuses—for the behaviors, personalities, and achievements, or lack thereof, of their offspring. Sometimes we call out the schools and churches that "didn't do their job." Or some dads and moms have succumbed to this grandest of excuses: He got in with the wrong crowd!

The only place we can find real answers is in that proverbial mirror. To understand what it means to be an accountable parent, we need to understand what an *un*accountable parent sounds like and make sure we aren't making excuses like these:

Nobody taught me how to do this.
My mom and dad weren't good parents.
I'm too busy to know what my kids are always doing.
My spouse doesn't help out.
The schools don't do enough.
My kid's friends are nothing but trouble!

Sound familiar? Have you ever said them to yourself or out loud? It's easy to do, we understand. However, parenting the QBQ way requires us to be No Excuses parents. This means becoming the dad or mom who believes deeply that when it comes to my child—*I own the result.*

Making excuses prevents us from solving problems, enhancing relationships, and from learning. Not to mention, we transfer the character flaw of making excuses to our kids!

Have you witnessed the "Circle of Blame"?

The mom or dad blames the child, who blames the friends, who blame their parents, who blame the teachers, who blame the taxpayers, who blame the government, who blames . . .

Well, okay, it's not really a circle, but you get the picture.

Karen was getting preschooler Molly and herself ready

to leave the house for a Bible study leader's meeting, when the phone rang. It was someone returning her call. Knowing that she didn't really have time to talk, Karen made the *choice* to answer the phone anyway. For a multitasking mom, it was all about checking one more item off her endless list of things to do.

The conversation ended and now it was time to rush! "Molly, get going!" "Move faster!" "We're going to be late!" *Oh, great*, Karen thought, *now Molly's throwing a tantrum and I'm yelling!*

Finally in the van, driving a bit too fast, Karen felt the excuses start to form in her mind: *I had so much to do this morning! My phone conversation took too long! The three-year-old didn't cooperate!*

As the excuses came, her tension grew.

But then, just as those negative thoughts were clouding her thinking, like brilliant sunshine breaking through a dark sky she had *new* thoughts: *I chose to take the call. I chose to talk too long. I chose to be late.*

Karen's stress eased. Her mood lightened. She felt calm and ready to walk into the meeting and simply say to a dozen other moms, "I'm sorry I'm late."

*No excuses.*

So often parents admonish kids to "Make good choices!" and that's excellent guidance, for sure. But we must remember the QBQs that *moms and dads* need to ask like "How can *I* make better choices in my life?" and "What can *I* do to own my decisions?"

When appraising your own parenting, ask yourself if you've let blame creep into your parenting and your family. How far will our children—or we, for that matter—get in life traveling the lower road of excuse making? Not very far. There is a higher path called *personal accountability*, and each family member can take it. But that will happen only when Mom and Dad lead the way by practicing No Excuses parenting.

# CHAPTER ELEVEN

# Parental Abdication

*Today's parents tend to be more passive and less involved
in their children's lives than any generation in our
nation's history. They have turned their children over to
artificial, surrogate parents.*

—JOHN MACARTHUR

Kristin, our oldest, served as a youth mentor at a church
that held weekly meetings throughout the school year. One
evening, as fifteen-year-old Tina, one of Kristin's charges,
was hopping out of her mom's car at the youth center, Kristin
walked up to say hello. She and Tina's mom chatted briefly
about what the teens were doing that night. As Kristin
walked away with Tina, the mother shouted through the
open car window, "Oh, Kristin, would you talk to Tina about
her choice in friends?"

Now, Kristin, like anyone who works with teenagers,
loves to help them navigate life. But isn't holding a critical
conversation like that with the daughter the *parent's* job?

We all know that if the mother truly needed Kristin's collaboration, the request for help should have been in private.

Any youth mentor will tell you that often the mentor can sometimes have a more candid conversation with a teen than a parent. However, far too often parents leave these crucial conversations *solely* to the youth mentor (or other counselors, teachers, etc.). But that's not the lesson here. The point of this story is about the prevalence of parental abdication, which is a not-so-distant relative of blame and excuse making.

Parents who abdicate their leadership role at home ask IQs like these:

"Why doesn't someone deal with the problem of
    school bullying?"
"Who's going to teach kids about Internet
    safety?"
"When will the schools provide more character-
    building programs?"
"Why isn't there more effort to educate kids on the
    dangers of drugs?"

Outstanding moms and dads know that Brownie, Boy Scout, Girl Scout, and 4-H leaders, along with clergy, coaches, school counselors, aunts, uncles, and grandparents, can be terrific helpmates in the raising of a child. But, in the end, accountable parents grasp the truth that it is *their* job to bring their child successfully into adulthood. If at any moment we were to enter the home of a parent who refuses to abdicate their leadership role and ask, "Whose job is it to raise these kids?," the response would most certainly be "It's mine!"

# CHAPTER TWELVE

# They're Watching Us

*Children have never been very good at listening to their elders, but they have never failed to imitate them.*

—JAMES BALDWIN

**H**earing the phone ring, the parent yells to the eight-year-old, "Tell them I'm not home!"

A decade later, the parent yells at the eighteen-year-old, "Where did you learn to lie?"

Here's an unyielding, never-changing principle:

**Modeling is the most powerful of all teachers.**

So often we hear people blame Hollywood celebrities, politicians, and famous athletes for being poor role models. "How dare famous people fall off their pedestals and fail our kid," they lament. (Of course, these are pedestals that *we* should never have put them on in the first place.) Some parents even point fingers at teachers, coaches, clergy, neighbors, relatives, and family friends for "setting a poor example."

Who is *the* most critical role model for your child? Any answer other than "Me!" is a form of blame. Parenting with QBQ does not include using other people as excuses for what our child is or becomes. The outstanding parent who knows who the real role model is for their child asks the QBQ "How can I set a better example today?"

Here's an idea: Before we worry about the negative impact those outside our families might have on our children, let's consider:

If I don't want my kid to text while he drives, I'd better not do it myself.

If I don't want my kid to go to R-rated movies, I should not see them, either.

If I don't want my kid using foul words, I might want to keep my language in check.

If I don't want my kid to complain about others, I should temper my own criticisms.

If I don't want my kid to blame, I shouldn't scream at the ref during the Little League game.

If I want my kid to get more exercise, I better dust off my bicycle and take a ride.

If I want my kid to be friendly and outgoing, I should go meet the new neighbors.

If I want my kid to handle money well, I need to do the same.

Identify the behaviors you want your child to exhibit and then ask The Question *Behind* the Question: "What can I do today to engage in these behaviors in my life?"

Remember, they're watching us.

# CHAPTER THIRTEEN

# Never Forget the "I"

*Do not judge others, and you will not be judged. For you will be treated as you treat others. The standard you use in judging is the standard by which you will be judged. And why worry about a speck in your friend's eye when you have a log in your own?*

—MATTHEW 7:1-3 NLT

Who is the only person you can change?

If you're thinking, *Me*, then you are a wise person. But here's another key question: As you've been reading this material, have you also been picturing who you think *really* needs this book?

If you have been thinking, *So-and-so needs to read this!* then you are not alone. An interesting aspect of this message of personal accountability is that most people are for it, but more often than not people are for *other people* practicing it. Wives want husbands to hear it; husbands want wives to hear it; managers want employees to hear it; and friends want friends to hear it—and so on and so on.

Here's a principle that some find hard to accept, but we believe is very much true:

**We tend to teach to others what we
need to hear ourselves.**

When John asks twentysomething Molly, "Does everything
have to be a debate? Can't you sometimes just go along to get
along?" he knows that Molly's face—at that moment in
time—is his mirror.

And when Karen asks twentysomething Michael, "When
are you going to manage your time better?"—Michael's face
is *her* mirror.

However, there is a solution to this all-too-human phenomenon of trying to change others. . . .

Have you noticed that every QBQ we've presented so far
not only begins with "What" or "How"—the first of three
guidelines covered in Chapter Three—but also contains the
personal pronoun "I"? Plus, each Incorrect Question posed
*lacks* an "I"! And why is this? Because, as much as we'd like
to think otherwise, *I can only change me.* Period.

No, dads, you can't make your son who wants to be a
whitewater rafting guide come work at your corporation.

No, moms, you can't make your daughter be in the
marching band if she'd rather be on the field as the place-
kicker for the football team.

And no, parents, you can't change each other—so don't
bother trying.

We are often asked by dads and moms, "How do I *make*

my child be accountable?" On the surface, it seems like a reasonable question, but the answer is one that most parents don't want to hear: You can't. Yes, we can communicate expectations more clearly, impose fair consequences for "nonperformance," and follow through in a firm and consistent manner—all important parenting practices that have the potential to shape our kids' thinking and behaviors. But nobody can *make* anybody else—from deep within themselves—feel personally accountable for anything.

The better approach for parents is to first work on themselves by asking questions that contain the word "I" like "How can *I* change me?" "What can *I* do to learn new skills?" and "How can *I* develop effective parenting practices?"

So remember, when creating and asking QBQs, never forget the "I." The truth that I can only change me is the essence of personal accountability and the QBQ.

# CHAPTER FOURTEEN

# Life *Is* Fair

*Comfort and prosperity have never enriched the world
as much as adversity has.*
—BILLY GRAHAM

There are some stories that truly help us all understand the power of personal accountability. This one comes from our friend and associate Kevin Brown, who thoroughly knows the QBQ and how to apply it.

"Mr. and Mrs. Brown, your son has autism."

The doctor's words pierced the silence and took aim at our hearts. She continued, "Autism is a neurological disorder that affects nearly one out of one hundred fifty children. . . ."

The rest of her words fell on deaf ears. My brain was too busy asking questions like:

"Why is this happening to us?"

"Who will pay for the treatments?"

"When will this all go away?"

"Why is life so unfair?!"

I was angry.

After the initial shock wore off, my wife, Lisa, and I began learning everything we could about autism. It was an arduous process. There were times when we wanted to give up. There were times when the stress and frustration between us was palpable. We didn't always agree on which path to take. Our marriage was taxed. I would be lying if I said there weren't moments when I felt sorry for us. Our son, Josh, would never have the life we had imagined for him.

That was nine years ago. It hasn't been an easy road, but now when parents of special-needs children ask us for our "secrets to success," we tell them this:

There are no secrets.

Special-needs children, like all children, need a loving home where they can be equipped for life. Our job as Josh's parents is to help him become everything God made him to be. Lisa and I have discovered that it's a daily decision to take accountability for the results of our parenting. Every single day we have to resist the temptation to blame and become victims. The world of special-needs parenting is full of people ready to point the long finger of blame at the educational system, the doctors, the pharmaceutical companies, and society at large. "It's everyone else's fault and someone has to pay!" they say. We understand their frustration and pain, but all the blame game does is waste time and energy. It's our belief that we need to ask the QBQ "How can I be the best parent I can be?" because that's what *Josh* needs most.

We know there will always be people who say, "But life isn't fair!" Well, our feeling is this: Life *is* fair . . . because bad things can happen to *anyone*. The difference is always in what we choose to do about it.

When Lisa and I see that we're about to slide down the slippery slopes of blame, victim thinking, and procrastination, when we're stressed out, freaked out, and feeling overwhelmed—we reach into our parenting toolbox for the QBQ. By asking better questions like "How can I be more patient?," "What can I do to keep learning?," and "How can I support my spouse?" we are not only making better choices, we're putting ourselves back on the path of personal accountability.

# CHAPTER FIFTEEN

# QBQ Humility

*Humility and knowledge in poor clothes excel pride and ignorance in costly attire.*

—WILLIAM PENN

Derek, a twenty-year-old family friend, was hanging out at our house. Since we know him well, we could tell something was bothering him. When we asked what was going on, he just blurted out, "My dad—he's just so frustrating!" And then he told us this story:

Last night my father had an old college buddy, Bruce, over for dinner. After we finished eating, the three of us were hanging out at the kitchen table when Bruce started laughing about something my father said and accused him of being a prideful guy. Smiling and grimacing at the same time, my dad said, "What? Me prideful? No way!" Then he looked at me and asked, "Derek, am I prideful?"

So I quickly responded, "I really would rather not get involved here." But he came back with, "No, it's okay, really. What do you think?"

"Okay, well, yes—you can be. I mean, I've never heard you admit you're wrong about anything."

After a tense moment, my father said, "You know, son, I could make a list of your faults, too."

Ouch.

Maybe Derek's dad felt cornered. Maybe he was embarrassed. Or maybe he really *is* prideful. We'll never know what drove the retort, but at the very least, his response lacked a key quality of effective parenting: humility.

An essential principle in QBQ parenting is this: Humility is the cornerstone of leadership.

Without a doubt, being a mom or dad is the most critical leadership role one can hold, and as leaders, Cory in Chapter Three and Sheri in Chapter Four displayed humility perfectly when they asked their children, "What can I do to be a better dad for you?" and "How can I be a better mom for you right now?"

There is simply no better way to show humility in parenting than asking questions such as "How can I improve?" and "What can I do differently?"

Along with asking QBQs, accountable parents model humility by using the magic words for developing and maintaining a healthy relationship: "I'm sorry." They don't expect their children to apologize if they never do so themselves.

Humility and contrition are foundational to parenting the QBQ way, and it's simply vital that we bring them to our families. A little "I'm sorry, I was wrong. I don't know everything!" goes a long way.

Here are some humble QBQs to ask: "How can I build a better relationship with my child?" and "What can I do to demonstrate true humility to those around me?"

# CHAPTER SIXTEEN

# Be Present

*In bringing up children, spend on them half as much
money and twice as much time.*

—AUTHOR UNKNOWN

Tara was weeks from graduating from college when John took her out to lunch. During the conversation, he somewhat facetiously asked her if as an adult she could pinpoint what he might've done better as a dad. He added, with a big smile, "Tara, is there anything I do that exasperates you?"

"Well," she responded, "sometimes when I talk to you I'm not sure you're here. I wish you could really be with me when we're together."

*Oh.*

Being present. Definitely what moms and dads need to do—yet we have all kinds of excuses for not doing so.

I need to vacuum the living room.

I have to finish up this report.

I want to watch the big game.

I must send this one last email!

Sometimes parents ask the IQs "Why doesn't my daughter talk to me?" and "When will my son tell me what's going on in his life?" They're easy to ask, we know. We also know that most parents *want* to connect with their children, but they get in their own way.

During a workshop on the *Outstanding!* book, there was a lot of discussion about the chapter on listening. The concept of "multitasking" came up, and Tad, a thirtysomething husband and father, sheepishly admitted, "Oh, man, do I ever do that to my wife and kids. When I come home from work and they all want to tell me about their day, I lean against the kitchen counter checking email on my smart phone! I admit I don't catch much of what they say."

The truth is everyone "multitasks" in some way, but here's the problem with it:

**The mind can only hold one thought at a time.**

Some people can't accept that concept because the mind moves so quickly from one thing to another, it's easy to think that we really are doing many things well all at once. The reality is we're probably not doing *anything* well at that moment.

And we are surely not *being present*.

In part, the bad habits we've allowed to creep into our lives create a challenge to being present with our kids. More important, we too often fail to understand that it's *our job* to be—to the extent that we can—truly available to them. If we accept this responsibility as parents, then we must accept this truth: Children talk to us when *they* want to talk to us, and their sharing is not always on our timetable!

In the Miller home, just as the old folks are heading to bed, the teenager often starts to share—even though we've been together all evening long! And sometimes, when we think we've simply asked one of our kids to help us paint a room or landscape the yard, what we really have created is a safe opportunity for them to talk with us about what's happening in their world while working side by side.

Being together, working together, and engaging in shared activities all make it possible to be present and listen well. Some families, however, have erected barriers to connecting with each other within the home. Children are allowed to spend hours upon hours alone in their rooms, dinners are haphazard and on-the-go, and families rarely come together to enjoy a mutual activity. It's difficult to be present with each other when we're not with each other in the first place!

According to one couple, it was a blessing in disguise when their twelve-year-old son got into a bit of trouble. They chose to confiscate his many technology devices for a while, which left him with little to do except homework and interact with his parents. Two days later he told them he was enjoying hanging out with them and said they were "pretty cool" after all.

Now that's a compliment!

In the end, accountable parents choose to be present with their children, knowing that *the whole family will benefit*. They ask QBQs like "How can I listen more effectively?" and "What can I do to better connect with my child?"

Parents are busy people. We understand that. But let's both make and fulfill the important promise to our kids that when they talk to us, we'll be there.

# CHAPTER SEVENTEEN

# Becoming a Strong Parent

*If we don't shape our kids, they will be shaped by outside
forces that don't care what shape our kids are in.*

—DR. LOUISE HART

**Y**ears ago there was a show on television called *Charles in
Charge*. Many of today's moms and dads saw it as kids,
watched it in reruns, or at least have heard of it. Sadly, there
are parents now that could title their family *Child in Charge*.

We had just settled in at our favorite Olive Garden restaurant when we noticed a couple with their toddler sitting
nearby. In his little hands he clutched a solid rubber toy air-
plane. As the server was taking our drink order, a loud noise
commanded our attention. Turning toward the young family, we saw the little boy raise the toy high above his head
and bring it down against the table's surface with such force
that his parents' water glasses quivered and other patrons
looked their way. Then, like a blacksmith wielding his tool
over an anvil, the little guy lifted the toy plane and slammed

it into the table again, all the while yelling at the top of his lungs.

Meanwhile, the adults seated with him—looking frustrated and a tad embarrassed—avoided eye contact with other guests. But they also did little to stop the commotion.

While we were thinking that it was time to take the toy away and whisper into his adorable face a firm "No"—and maybe deliver him to the lobby for a mind-calming "time-out"—he dropped the plane onto the floor. Employing all the behaviors a toddler uses to get what he wants, he began to throw a mini-tantrum. Any hopes we had that the racket was about to end were dashed when his mom retrieved the toy and began "flying" it through the air while making aircraft noises and "landed" the plane back into her son's hands. He then lifted it to the sky and banged it on the table once more.

Who's in charge here?

One thing we know is this: All parents parent differently. There are varying styles, approaches, beliefs, and values. No two families are the same, and this is especially true when it comes to shaping a child's behavior. Or said in a more unfashionable way: *discipline*. Certainly it's not our place to judge whether other parents discipline their children in a right or wrong manner. However, at the risk of oversimplifying what might be a very complex and contentious issue, we would like to suggest that when it comes to the topic of discipline, there are two types of parenting: weak and strong.

The story of the hammering toddler is one of *weak* parenting. Simply put, the child was "ruling the roost" with permission granted by his mom and dad. As the little boy freely engaged in his chosen behavior—at that moment—he was the "boss of him." Essentially, Dad and Mom had abdicated their leadership roles as parents.

Then there is *strong* parenting, characterized by a consistently *loving but firm* approach that instructs children that the parent is the key authority figure in their world. Strong parents understand that the fundamental purpose of disciplining is, over time, to create *self*-discipline within the child. They don't abandon this responsibility by using excuses such as "I'm too tired" or "It's inconvenient right now" or "It's just too hard." Furthermore, they would never say, "I don't know how to discipline" because strong parents know that strong parenting can be learned.

The reality is this: Most parents would *say* that loving discipline is a good thing, but *doing* it is another matter. We find that the problem for many parents is not *how* to discipline (though that's important) but possessing the *desire to discipline* and knowing *when to discipline*. This is what interests us most: helping parents want to engage in strong parenting and really grasp the timing for doing so. When it comes to learning the "how to" aspects of effective discipline, there are books, podcasts, websites, and classes galore that can guide parents in which specific techniques and methods to apply. Please, immerse yourself in the many resources available to parents today.

A mom's or dad's desire to discipline is rooted in knowing that our children are a product of us and that we are personally accountable *to* them to be the best parent we can be. Strong parents know that it's their job—the one they chose—to firmly shape their child as he or she grows. They know that though disciplining may be exhausting and time-consuming, there will be benefits reaped for all involved. Bottom line, outstanding parents discipline themselves to discipline the child. They are not afraid to be firm because they know *it's the right thing to do.*

Regarding *when* to discipline, we suggest any mom or dad use the "Discipline D's" to steer them in knowing when it's time to be a strong parent. For parents who want to engage in purposeful, timely, and effective discipline, here are some key questions to ask when the situation calls for their use:

Disobedient: Is my child disobeying an authority figure?
Destructive: Is my child damaging property?
Distracting: Is my child interrupting others' concentration?

Disruptive: Is my child upsetting the environment?

Dangerous: Is my child at risk or putting others at risk?

Disrespectful: Is my child showing disregard for people?

"Yes" answers to any of these questions tell us it's time to demonstrate strong, accountable parenting. So instead of asking an Incorrect Question that sounds anything like "Why won't my child behave?" let's ask QBQs like:

"What can I do to learn new parenting skills?"

"How can I earn my child's respect?"

"What can I do to better understand the role of a strong parent?"

# CHAPTER EIGHTEEN

# Do the Hard Stuff

*Let us not become weary in doing good, for at the proper
time we will reap a harvest if we do not give up.*

—GALATIANS 6:9 NIV

"Why is my daughter so disobedient?"
"When will my son stop driving me crazy?"
"Who will save me from these children?!"

When parents ask IQs like these—essentially "Why is my
child so out of control?"—the answer could be because *the
parent* is not in control. The evidence that your son or daughter has become your boss is clear to everyone if:

Your child constantly interrupts you when you're
chatting with other people.
Your kid whines enough to know that your "No"
will eventually turn into a "Yes."
You make excuses for bad behavior, everything
from "She's tired!" to "He's strong-willed!"

When you tell your children not to do something,
they do it anyway because your follow-through
stinks.

Your son or daughter is allowed to speak to you dis-
respectfully.

Any penalties that you impose for misbehaving are
lifted early or never enforced.

It's a given that we love our kids, worry for them, and want
them to succeed in life. We show our love by striving to keep
them safe from fast cars, hot stoves, and creepy strangers.
But QBQ parents also demonstrate love for their child by *not*
engaging in the weak parenting scenarios described above.
It takes both diligence and vigilance to be a strong, accountable mom or dad, but that's okay because no parent had children to avoid work and inconvenience!

Be a strong parent. Do the hard stuff now.

# CHAPTER NINETEEN

# Strong Parenting Begins with Strong Values

*The virtue of a man ought to be measured, not by his extraordinary exertions, but by his everyday conduct.*

—BLAISE PASCAL

When Karen was young, her dad often asked, "Have you called your grandmother lately?" It was his way of saying to Karen that staying in touch with her parents' parents was important to him, something he valued. Adopting his value, Karen has encouraged our kids to do the same.

Parents do a lot of important things, but maybe none as critical as passing on their values. And the secret to passing our values on is consistency, repetition—and finding those "teachable moments."

Terri and Brady are strong, effective parents who more than anything want to infuse their values into their children. One day, Morgan, their oldest and in middle school—a time when children are figuring out what their parents, peers, and they value—came to Terri and asked if she could go to a movie with her friends. As it turned out, Morgan's friends

were already at the nearby theater *and* they'd bought her a
ticket! Morgan pleaded with her mom to let her go. Giving
lots of reasons why she should be allowed, she added, "It's
only rated PG-13."

Terri then took Morgan to the computer where they
looked up the movie on a site that helps parents discern
which movies are appropriate. After they had both read
exactly what gave the movie its rating, Terri turned to Morgan and asked her what she thought.

"Do you think based on what we believe and value in
our family that this is a movie you should go see?"

Morgan whined a bit more but then concluded, "No, I
should skip it."

Was she embarrassed when she told her friends she
couldn't go? Yes. But, as an accountable parent, Terri used
this teachable moment as an opportunity to both affirm Morgan's feelings *and* uphold the values of their family—not
always an easy thing to do.

All parents value different principles, actions, and forms
of "success." For example, we feel that youth sports are
mostly about learning skills, getting exercise, building relationships, and understanding the power of teamwork. Other
parents believe youth sports are about winning. That's okay,
we have different values. This is why you'll see a bumper
sticker that exclaims "Proud parent of an honor student"
while the next one screams from the car ahead of us: "My kid

plays varsity football!" To be honest, two we'd love to see are "My kid has great manners!" and "My child is respectful!"

Yes, we all have different values. It's certainly not our place to tell anyone what to value, but we do say be certain of your values, share your values, and live them yourself. Of course, a key component of all of this is the defining of our "absolutes." These are the principles and behaviors that a strong parent is "black and white" about. Examples we've seen in values-driven families are no R-rated movies, no cussing, and no hitting. On the flip side, exhibiting excellent manners, kindness to guests, and verbal respect to each other are required. Absolutes like these make it easier for parents and children to make wise decisions and choices. They become tools that guide us, so to speak, in all we do.

Here are some QBQs to ask:

"What can I do to be clear on what I value?"
"How can I better teach my values to my child?"
"What can I do to coach my kids in making good
    choices?"
"How can I define my 'absolutes'?"

# CHAPTER TWENTY

# No Enabling Allowed

*In the end, it's not what you do for your children, but
what you've taught them to do for themselves.*

—ANN LANDERS

A mother of two confessed to Karen, "I think I've taught
my daughter a bad thing."

She continued, "I am constantly on her to clean her room,
and when I got really mad and said to her, 'Why don't you
just get it done when I ask?' my daughter calmly replied,
'Why should I? I know that after you've told me to do something twice, you'll just do it yourself.'"

Weak parents enable their kids. They let them off the
hook or cover for them—doing the mental, emotional, and
physical work that *they* should be doing themselves.

Many parents want to be their children's cheerleader,
consistently sending them an "I'm on your side!" message—
but this approach to parenting can be taken to a level of
unhealthy enabling. When one girl in our daughter's high
school was suspended for fighting, her mother came to the

principal's office and yelled so loudly at the administrator that the students could hear her voice echoing up and down the halls.

The truth is, strong parents support their children but let them experience the consequences of their own actions and "fight their own battles."

Now, if our three-year-old is being bullied by a four-year-old at the park, we step in. This is not the time to be a passive observer while thinking, *Hmm, let's see how he handles this.* But somewhere along the parenting journey, effective parents begin to understand when to step back and let their child make a mistake, solve a problem, or handle a relational struggle. If we don't do this, how will they grow? Effective parents know that failure is an inherent part of the growth process and, at times, they let their kid fail.

There are many reasons why some parents enable their children, but let's simply focus on solutions by asking QBQs like "What can I do to help my child grow?" and "How can I discover ways to support my child without enabling?"

One surefire way to "cease and desist" is by learning to spot a child's excuse-making a mile away. We've talked about being the No Excuses parent *and* about being the role model for our kids. Not only do moms and dads need to eliminate excuses from their parenting and refuse to indulge in blame, we must not *accept* excuses from our children. Every time we accept excuses from our children, we've taught them to play victim, procrastinate, and point fingers. And the outcome is a bad one: a young person who fails to take responsibility for his or her own actions and refuses to take ownership of the consequences of those actions.

Our daughter Jazzy is an outstanding student. She wants to excel and usually does. But when she received a disappointing mark on an eighth-grade science exam, the first words out of her mouth were, "It wasn't a fair test!" When we asked what she meant, she said, "I thought the teacher would cover different terms than the ones she chose."

So, because *she* failed to properly prepare for the exam, *it's the teacher's fault*?

"Jazz," we told her, "you need to know *all* the material."

Parents can stop the unhealthy cycle of enabling when they allow the natural consequences of their child's actions to occur. Again, if a child's safety is at risk—like a toddler running toward a busy street—we get involved, fast! But if our twelve-year-old has put off creating that science project poster board until the night before it's due, the QBQ parent does *not* rescue the child. If our child gets a bad grade, so be it. But along with the disappointing result, there will be a lesson learned—a lesson that just might cause them to do it right the next time.

The truth is this: QBQ parents let their children fail, don't lie or cover for them, and certainly never make or accept excuses for their kids' behavior. For their sake and ours, let's ask, "What can I do to allow my children to learn from their mistakes?" and "How can I help my children 'own' their results?"

When we have raised accountable children who are willing and able to say, "I own it!" then we have truly done our job raising great kids.

# Chapter Twenty-one

# Elevate Your Expectations

*Being classy is my teenage rebellion.*

—REBECCA MCKINSEY

It was time for our daughter Tara to take a driver's education class. When they were registering for the course, Karen and Tara met the instructor for the first time. After introductions, he turned to Tara and asked, "Do you drink?"

Tara, surprised by the question, immediately said, "No."

The instructor responded, "You will. Have you tried drugs?"

Again, "No!"

And the guy said again, "You will. Do you party?"

Disbelieving, Karen asked, "Is there some reason you're asking all these questions?"

The man responded, "All teenagers do these things."

After an uncomfortable moment or two, Karen and Tara politely excused themselves, headed to the car—and never returned.

We're not surprised if you're thinking, *What's with this guy?* Or possibly you're thinking, *He's right!*

Well, we actually think he's wrong. In our opinion, this man has not only bought into the stereotypes people routinely accept about our youth, he's a propagator of them.

You've probably heard statements like these:

"All teenagers are rude and disrespectful."

"Teens are lazy and don't want to work."

"Every teenager rebels."

"All teens will have sex before marriage."

"Teenagers only want to party."

If we let these untruths creep into our parenting, we fail everyone. Yes, growing up can be challenging and the teen years can be a struggle for some, but we should not use these facts as excuses not to parent in a strong fashion. It's our job to call our kids to a higher level of conduct, and it can be done.

We believe that *wisdom is what we learn after we know it all.* So after parenting for a lot of years, we feel that we can offer this guidance to all dads and moms: Choose your battles. Not everything that comes our way is worth the time, effort, and energy to fight. However, we can say from the heart that fighting the stereotypes society promotes about young people today is definitely a battle worth choosing.

Our daughter Kristin shared this story:

When my sister Tara was eleven and I had just turned thirteen, we fought a lot. We're friends now, but back then . . . *watch out!* One day we had a fight where I said some mean things, Tara responded in kind, and then she started crying. I rolled my eyes at her, ran down the hall, and slammed my bedroom door—*hard*. And what did Tara do? She told Mom.

So Mom sat us both down at the kitchen table for what we both presumed would be a lecture. My bad attitude was demonstrated by crossed arms and averted eyes. Next to me, Tara just sniffled.

Mom looked at us and immediately my attention was piqued. She didn't yell, nor did she list all the things we'd done that were wrong. Looking back many years now, she used our spat as an opportunity to share wisdom.

"You know what, girls? Dad and I are not going to tolerate this kind of stuff. You're both entering the time of life when society says you will be disrespectful, stubborn, and selfish. You are going through a lot of changes, and the world is going to tell you how you should be, how *all* teenagers act. I want to tell you both—you don't have to be these things. You can choose to conform to the stereotypes of teens, or you can rise above and be different. Of course, life with Mom and Dad will be a lot easier if you *don't* conform."

And as disinterested as I tried to look that day, Mom had struck a chord. I wanted to be different, and Tara did, too. It's true, just because someone turns thirteen doesn't mean they have to suddenly hate their parents, complain about how unfair life is, and have an "attitude." Our mom's lesson was a good one.

The reality is our children often become what we expect of them. So wouldn't it be best for parents to aim high in their expectations? It's quite likely that *they will respond*. Outstanding parents don't passively accept the world's stereotypes about young people. Knowing that the answers are always in the questions, they ask these QBQs: "How can I best support my kids while not buying into the stereotypes of the world?" and "What can I do to elevate my expectations and communicate them to my child?"

# CHAPTER TWENTY-TWO

# QBQ Encouragement

*Do not let any unwholesome talk come out of your*
*mouths, but only what is helpful for building others*
*up according to their needs, that it may benefit those*
*who listen.*

—EPHESIANS 4:29 NIV

About to run his first race, the young man said to his mother, "You mean, Mom, if I really believe in myself, I can win this race?" She responded wisely, "Son, if you believe in yourself, you've already won."

Encouragement. Good stuff. And the age of the child doesn't matter.

More than twenty years after Karen left home, her mom told her, "You're so good with the elderly—I've seen it. Maybe you should volunteer at a long-term-care center." Karen admits to beaming just a bit when her mom made that comment. She remembers how good those words felt.

If encouraging words feel good to a mom of seven from *her* mom, just think what they mean to kids while we're still helping them mature into adulthood.

One winter evening in 1976, John was on the wrestling

mat at his high school in Ithaca, New York, competing in a six-minute match. In front of a big crowd including his dad, Jimmy Miller, who was the Cornell University wrestling coach, John was winning handily against a younger opponent. By the end of the first two-minute period he was ahead 11 to 2!

But in the opening moments of the second period, John made a big tactical error and before he knew it he was on his back with the other boy squarely on top of him. The referee slapped the mat and it was over. John, a senior and the team captain, had been pinned by a . . . *tenth grader!*

The home crowd was stunned. John was devastated.

Later that evening, as John and his father were leaving the gym, Cheryl, a junior, approached excitedly with that night's program and a pen in hand. She asked John to give her his autograph. He did, somewhat reluctantly. *Why would she want a loser to sign her program?*

After Cheryl left, it was only John and Jimmy. With perfect timing, John's father said something that is still imprinted on John's mind today: "You know, Johnny, that gal sees you as a hero tonight *simply because you're you.*"

With those well-timed words, Jimmy helped John lift himself up when he was down—and John has never forgotten it.

Encouraging our children doesn't mean showering them with hollow praise. The objective is not to reward failure, or even mediocrity. Understanding this, when it comes to lifting your child up, you need to decide what you'll say and when and how you'll say it—but quite honestly, most parents need to encourage more.

A mom who is working very hard to learn new parenting skills shared with us a mistake she now realizes she made. Her daughter brought home a report card featuring five A's and one B- and the mom recalled letting this slip out of her mouth: "But, honey, we know you can do better."

Sounds a lot like the father whose son reported he'd finished mowing the lawn and only heard back, "Did you sweep off the sidewalk?"

Or the parent who lets their preschooler set the table or make the bed for the first time, but follows right along after them correcting their work and showing the child "how to do it right."

Strong, accountable parents understand the power of parental praise. They know that words of encouragement spoken to a child can last a lifetime. It's these moms and dads who ask QBQs like "How can I become a more encouraging parent?" and "What can I do to lift my child up today?"

# CHAPTER TWENTY-THREE

# Let Them Be Them

*To be yourself in a world that is constantly trying to
make you something else is the greatest accomplishment.*
—RALPH WALDO EMERSON

During a QBQ workshop with a dozen CEOs from different companies, one of the participants announced, "I'm going
to take my son around the world in two weeks. He just grad-
uated from Yale!" John thought to himself, *How terrific to
share time together, celebrating the son's graduation from college,
just father and son.* John was then somewhat taken aback by
the CEO's next comment:

"Yep, I'm taking him around the world so I can talk him
into joining the family business!"

Parenting isn't easy and kids don't come with instruction
manuals. We grow into the job daily—if we choose to. Or, we
can make common parental mistakes, such as attempting to
make our children be what we want them to be.

There is a story about our only son, Michael, in *Flipping
the Switch*. Because John has a wrestling background and

Karen loves watching the sport, we both thought Michael would wrestle. But we knew there was no hope for another generation of Miller wrestlers when John took eight-year-old Michael to his first and only wrestling practice. When her "men" returned home that evening, Karen asked Michael, "How'd it go? Did you have fun?" He quickly wrinkled his nose and said, "Mom, did you know those other boys are sweaty?!"

It was over. He'd never set foot on a wrestling mat again. However, because of his theatrical, musical, and comedic talents, we found ourselves watching him onstage instead.

After John shared this story with an audience, a woman came up to him and said, "I sure wish my nephew could learn the QBQ."

When John inquired why, she said, "Because my nephew has a sixteen-year-old boy who wants to play the oboe, but his dad wants him to play football. And since he won't, my nephew calls his son a 'pansy.'"

There are consequences when parents engage in name-calling in the misguided hope of motivating their children. At the very least, children may be embarrassed. But there's a real risk of destroying their belief in themselves, along with permanently damaging the relationship with their parents. Believing that one person can change another is a fundamental mistake.

When it comes to helping a child determine his or her

course in life, accountable parents know that if they've laid a foundation of strong values within their child, all they need to do is ask QBQs such as:

> "What can I do to get to know my child better?"
> "How can I encourage my kids to find their own way?"
> "How can I be excited about what excites my child?"
> "What can I do to help my daughter use her gifts?"
> "How can I help my son realize his dreams?"
> "What can I do to treat each of my children as the individual they are?"

Asking questions like these is the same as making the commitment never to push our children to choose any path *but their own.*

# CHAPTER TWENTY-FOUR

# Flipping the Switch

*Too often we give children answers to remember rather
than problems to solve.*

—ROGER LEWIN

John had just finished a speaking engagement in Mississippi based on his book *Flipping the Switch* when a woman whose name badge read "Sally" came up to say hello. At least, that's how John thought she'd start the conversation. It went more like this: "I've changed my thinking, and I'm done worrying about my daughter's backflip."

Slightly confused and tempted to blurt out "Huh?!" John said, "Pardon me. I'm sorry, would you mind beginning again, Sally?"

She responded, "As you began speaking, I was thinking about my eleven-year-old daughter who's in gymnastics, and I was hoping I'd hear some ideas on how to motivate her to get her backflip down. She just isn't getting it."

John smiled and asked, "Well, what did you come up with?"

Sally stood a little taller as she answered proudly, "It's not my job. That's her job. I just never saw it that way before."

Thankfully, Sally had "flipped the switch." Many parents believe it's their job to make a child want to succeed at a task or achieve a goal. In the long run, though, we are more successful at "letting them be them" when we come to embrace this healthy truth:

**A parent should not be more concerned about the child's success or failure than the child is.**

Please don't misunderstand, if our toddler is not speaking as well as we think he should be or our fourth grader is failing math, then it is normal and right for a parent to be intensely concerned. And, yes, coaching and guiding our children is certainly a core part of parenting. But there comes a time in the life of an outstanding parent, as our kids move toward adulthood, that we arrive at that place where we stop trying to make *our* goals *their* goals.

We really do know how tempting it is for a mom or dad to want a child to "get her backflip," but as Sally showed us, that switch can be flipped.

# CHAPTER TWENTY-FIVE

# Speak Well

*Keep your tongue from evil and*
*your lips from speaking lies.*

—PSALM 34:13

While out for dinner with Kristin, our son-in-law Erik, and their eighteen-month-old son, Joshua, we sat near a mom and dad and their son, an early teen. The contrast was striking. While they ate in peace, we ate *and* managed a toddler who had discovered the tantrum. At one point, Joshua reared back so hard he hit his head on the wall behind his chair and began screaming louder! We were pretty sure every person in the restaurant was watching—in a relieved sort of way—as Kristin took him outside to calm down.

While mom and son were gone, pleasantries were exchanged with the family next to us and a conversation began. Thinking they were going to tell us that they understood the challenge of babies (especially when out in public) and maybe express complete understanding, the mom pointed at her own child and said, "We'll trade you our teenager for that little guy any day of the week!"

Everyone laughed.

But the moment reminded Karen and me of a T-shirt we once saw that said, "Mothers of teenagers know why animals eat their young!"

These sorts of comments might seem funny at the time, but we suggest that making them is a habit we parents would do well to break. How does it serve the child, the parent, or anyone else when we utter statements like these?

"I can't wait for summer to end so my kids will be
 back in school and out of my hair!"
"You have three teen girls?! You must be going
 crazy!"
"Just dropped my preschooler off and I'm so glad to
 be away from him for a couple hours!"
"I hate these 'terrible twos'—she's driving me nuts
 with her tantrums!"
"You think your little boy is a handful now? Wait
 till he hits middle school!"

We're not trying to deny what might be real, nor do we want to minimize true parental frustrations. But remarks like these have many negative consequences. They tear children down, diminish our joy in parenting, interfere with a dad's or mom's desire to learn new skills, and might just undermine *other* parents' belief in their role and their children.

QBQ parents accept complete responsibility for every word that comes out of their mouths. No excuses! And they ask these accountable questions:

"What can I do to speak more positively?"
"How can I better understand the impact my words have on others?"
"What can I do to vent my frustration in a more constructive way?"

Bottom line: It's always better to be positive than negative. Let's discipline ourselves to speak well of the children.

# Chapter Twenty-six

# Team Family

*If the family were a boat, it would be a canoe that makes*
*no progress unless everyone paddles.*
—LETTY COTTIN POGREBIN

It seems that in many organizations—businesses, non-profits, churches, and social or athletic groups—people often say proudly, "We're like a family!" And when things change they bemoan, "We're not a family anymore!"

Interestingly, though, nobody in a family ever says, "We're like a sports team!" or "We're like a corporate sales department!"

So does this mean that families have cornered the market on teamwork and collaboration—ideals that are highly esteemed in the organizational world? Or does it simply mean that people have an idyllic view of families being closely knit groups where there is trust, caring, sharing, and a sense of community? A family is seen as a place where we can be vulnerable, safe from retribution and incrimination, where someone "has our back," members are free to speak their minds, and decisions are often made together.

Of course, not all families—or all teams—fit this description. However, just as an organizational "team leader" or an athletic team coach can ask a QBQ like "What can I do to help the team move forward?" parents can ask, "What can I do to build a stronger team within my home?"

At a school event in 2000, Karen was approached by her friend Kris, who shared that she had heard that the county was looking for a family to foster or adopt three sisters under the age of six. Kris, who had adopted children herself, knew we would be interested. Karen pondered this news.

Sitting with eleven-year-old Michael in the school auditorium, she scribbled a note to him: "Kris says there are three little girls who need a home." Mike read it, looked at Karen, and gave her a thumbs-up. Wondering if he really got it, Karen whispered to him, "Mike, three *girls*. That will make six sisters—and you!" Mike took the paper and pen from Karen and wrote: "Cool! Are we going to do it?"

The next day, we sat down with all four kids and explained that to do this we had to be a real team. Everyone had to be on board. With unanimous enthusiasm we moved forward. It hasn't been easy, but having the whole family vote YES! sure made the difference.

Teamwork—it's a family thing. So let's ask, "What can I do to encourage teamwork in my family?" and "How can I demonstrate my belief in the value of working together?"

# CHAPTER TWENTY-SEVEN

# Family Stress Is a Choice

*Stress is nothing more than a socially acceptable*
*form of mental illness.*
—RICHARD CARLSON

Marc, a regional manager for a specialty food products company, attended a *QBQ!* training workshop, and then emailed us this:

"When I showed up for the meeting, I wasn't only tired, I also felt down and discouraged. I was thinking maybe I needed a new job. Then I learned in the *QBQ!* session that 'stress is a choice' and I immediately recognized how true that statement is. It's not my staff, my boss, my customers, my coworkers, or my family who are creating stress in my life—it's *me!*"

Stress is a choice. Do you buy that? We hope so—because it's true. And by extension, we believe this:

**Family stress is a choice.**

Dance competitions. Travel soccer teams. Gymnastics three nights a week. Hockey practice at the crack of dawn on weekdays. Guitar and piano lessons Tuesday and Thursday evenings. Weekend-long tournaments. And, of course, end-of-year recitals. Not to mention . . . *schoolwork!*

Have you ever wanted to yell, "STOP THE MADNESS!!!"

We're not advocating abolishing youth activities. We know many good things happen when children participate in the right activity for them. We simply believe that parents should recognize that the stress a family experiences is created by the choices they make. Stress and tension (not to mention fatigue and exhaustion) don't happen *to* us—we do it to ourselves.

Too often we succumb to the pressure from our children's peer groups—and from our own peers—to get our kids into activities when they're young, and not always for the right reasons. Maybe we have that elusive college scholarship in mind or we want our child to be the star student, musician, actor, or athlete that we never were. We push our children and ourselves. But at what cost?

Possibly we are sacrificing our child's childhood. That may sound alarmist, but does that make it untrue?

When we moved to Denver in the late 1990s, we went door-to-door in our new neighborhood looking for kids who might be interested in playing with ours. But nobody was home. They were all at their after-school activities. And when they did get home, schoolwork took over. Nobody seemed to be taking the time to just play.

As retro as this may sound, is it possible there'd be value in getting back to more unscheduled time for shooting hoops in the driveway, dangling on backyard jungle gyms, or hitting a few balls, even with the occasional broken window involved?

Don't get us wrong, our family had its busyness. Each of our first four children had one core activity. Kristin sang in the choir, Tara danced, Michael participated in drama, and Molly played soccer. And our younger girls—Charlene, Jazzy, and Tasha—are involved in student council, National Honor Society, and gymnastics. But even with this fairly limited amount of extracurricular involvement, we've experienced seasons when various kids weren't home much and lacked time to "chillax" with the family.

It's simply our opinion that one of the best things a parent can learn to do is to say "no" when their child wants to be involved in one more thing. The truth is, when our kids are young it's hard to imagine them fully grown. Even though everyone says, "They'll be gone before you know it," in actuality only parents who've raised their kids to adulthood really comprehend that statement. When we're in the throes of parenting young children, it's almost impossible to grasp the fact that we're in the "sweet spot" of parenting *and it should be savored.*

The sweet spot of parenting is those years between diapers and driver's licenses. From the "Whose turn is it to change her this time?" phase to the waiting-up-at-night-for-a-teen-driver-to-come-home phase are the years when we really have them by our side to hold, to cherish, to teach, to guide—and to engage in play.

But we can't do much of this when they're not home.

Each family has to decide when too much outside activity is too much, but the secret to handling the stress—and there is stress inherent in all parenting—is to first recognize that *we* create it. Busyness and the stress that can come from it are choices we make. It does not come from external sources. Once we accept responsibility for our family's stress, we can ask QBQs like these:

"How can I get a handle on our busyness?"
"What can I do to create more time for fun?"
"How can I find greater joy in just being with my children?"

In this age of endless noise, distraction, and competition, let's reduce the stress in our families by remembering the incredible value of downtime and togetherness. Is it trite or true to say that we really do only have them at home for such a very short season? There aren't many parents of grown children who say, "I spent too much time with my kids when they were little!"

So grab your old baseball glove or, if you never had one yourself, go out and buy one today and play some catch with your child. Even if a window gets broken, you'll still be choosing a lot less stress.

# Chapter Twenty-eight

# Regrets No More

*It is impossible to live without failing at something,*
*unless you live so cautiously that you might as well not*
*have lived at all.*

—J. K. ROWLING

One humid summer evening, while living in Minnesota, we ventured out for a family bike ride, well aware of the danger. If you know the "Land of 10,000 Lakes," then you know the unofficial state bird is the mosquito.

Heading back to the house, we decided to take a shortcut using a path that went underneath large trees and through some mature bushes—a prime hangout for the dreaded blood-sucking pests. We knew this shortcut was risky, but felt that we could ride and glide fast enough to beat the bugs.

The path, which we'd nicknamed Mosquito Lane, took a small dip in the middle. The best way to get through it quickly—without red welts covering your body—was to gain momentum heading into it and use your speed to climb to freedom on the other side. It certainly wasn't a deep valley with steep sides at all—unless you're seven, like Tara, our dark-haired, dark-eyed child mosquito magnet.

We entered the sunless path, with Dad and a few Miller kids leading the way. Tara and Karen brought up the rear. Mom swiftly reached the other side and looked back to see that Tara, at the bottom of the dip, had made the worst mistake possible: *She had stopped.*

Climbing off her bicycle, Tara began to push it uphill. Karen watched incredulously as a cloud of the happiest mosquitoes in the world descended upon our little girl. And that's when Karen, in her own words, "lost it." Frustrated with her child doing the nonsensical—standing still, wasting time, swatting at the bugs instead of moving forward as fast as possible—she began to yell at the seven-year-old. Actually, it was more like a scream.

"Tara, what are you doing? Stop trying to hit them! Get back on your bike! Ride, Tara, ride!!!"

Finally grasping that Tara didn't know what to do, Karen jumped off her bike, ran down the hill, and grabbed Tara and her bike, yelling at her to get moving. When they got to the top of the rise, we were all mortified to see that Tara was literally covered with bug bites.

Regrets? You bet. Long after the event, Karen continued to ask herself unproductive questions like these:

"Why was I so impatient?"

"Why was I so harsh?"

"Why didn't I rescue her sooner?"

Regret. Every parent has it because every parent has failed to act, said the wrong thing or didn't say the right thing, made a less-than-stellar decision, and shown poor judgment. In other words, all moms and dads make mistakes.

Like the time John, during a Thanksgiving meal, tried to get six-year-old Charlene to eat creamed onions. But that's another story . . .

Understanding that regret solves no problems and moves nobody forward is not new, but that doesn't mean parents don't experience it. But it's our job to shed regrets as much as we can. Here's why:

### We can't be the best parent possible while reliving the past.

Now, as an adult, Tara has heard her mom say the words, "I'm sorry about that day. I wish I'd handled it differently."

When parents are aware enough *and* brave enough to bring mistakes up, put them on the table, and explore them with the child, it helps everyone move forward.

Today, both Mosquito Lane and the "Tale of the Creamed Onions" are Miller family history, and since "history" is always in the past, that's exactly where we want those mistakes to stay. Accountable dads and moms ask the QBQ, "What can I do to learn from and move beyond mistakes to be the best parent I can be—*right now*?"

# CHAPTER TWENTY-NINE

# Truth Builds Trust

*Truth has no special time of its own.*
*Its hour is now—always.*
—ALBERT SCHWEITZER

Some parents (who will remain unnamed) have seen the animated film *Aladdin* about one hundred times because they enjoyed it right along with the kiddos!

In two plot-twisting moments when Princess Jasmine is in a perilous situation, Aladdin is there, reaching out to her—stretching, straining, desperately trying to rescue her. But she hesitates. Then he looks into her eyes and asks, "Do you trust me?"

In a perfect Disney moment, Jasmine knows the answer. Her fear dissolves and she takes Aladdin's hand. She's safe— and we can breathe again.

"Do you trust me?" It's a question that strikes at the heart of all relationships. When we've built trust in our personal relationships, life is good.

Perhaps the most important way that QBQ parents can

build trust is by speaking the truth. They don't make empty threats, they don't "spin" messages to their kids, and they certainly never lie.

If your child needs a shot at the doctor's, then tell him that. If Muffy the cat had to be put down for health reasons, don't say she ran away. If you can't take the children to the zoo as promised due to an unexpected work conflict, don't tell them the zoo is closed!

As parents we need to remember that if truth builds trust, then the opposite is true as well: Lies destroy trust—and they create anxiety.

When we tell falsehoods to our kids, we create needless uncertainty and fear in them. Are there underlying psychological reasons for this that go deeper than we're going to go here? Yes. But we do know the solution and you do, too: Tell kids the truth as often as we can and our families will be built on an unshakable foundation of trust.

Here is a QBQ to ask: "What can I do to create more trust in my home?"

# CHAPTER THIRTY

# Trust Is Earned

*Trust, but verify.*

—RONALD REAGAN

Kids need to understand that they *never* have to earn our love, but they do need to earn our trust. So along with the parental responsibility of creating trust within the home through words and actions, a strong, accountable parent feels obligated to communicate this message to their child:

**If I can't trust you with the little things,
how can I trust you with the big things?**

Most parents readily accept this statement as valid, but when it comes to disciplining themselves to adhere to it, they find it's not so easy. In fact, it can be quite hard—for the parent! But parenting the QBQ way is not about convenience or avoiding making tough decisions. As parents, we are builders of people—and when we teach our kids that trust must be earned, we've given them a solid life foundation.

Marie told us about her sixteen-year-old son, Joey, who was failing Spanish. He was doing fine in all of his other courses, but needed to pass Spanish to graduate from high school. He hated the course and more often than not simply didn't turn in his work. He confessed to his mother that Spanish simply didn't interest him. But he sure was interested in something else: getting his driver's permit! Like most teen boys, he talked about it all the time. And Marie and her husband did want him to be able to drive. They could use a hand running his younger siblings around town to all of their activities!

But Marie is no weak parent. She told Joey, "Driving is not a right, it's a privilege. If I can't trust you to succeed in school, how can I trust you to drive a car? There will be no taking any driver's test until you get your act together in Spanish class."

Three weeks later, Joey had a C+ in Spanish on his way to a solid B in the course—all because Marie drew what we call "loving lines in the sand." It's amazing what strong, accountable parenting will do just by asking QBQs like these:

> "How can I create opportunities for my kids to
> prove their trustworthiness?"

"What actions can I take to give my child more
   responsibility as they are ready to handle it?"
"How can I better convey what's expected?"
"What can I do to remain strong in my parenting
   when challenged?"

# Chapter Thirty-one

# Blending Is Hard Work

*The great gift of family life is to be intimately acquainted*
*with people you might never even introduce yourself to,*
*had life not done it for you.*

—KENDALL HAILEY

Neil, a mid-fifties *QBQ!* fan from Wisconsin, sat down with us over lunch and shared his story. At forty, he married for the first time. His wife, previously married, had two boys, ages twelve and ten. They had met in Seattle where she already owned a home so, post-wedding, Neil moved in and joined his new family. But, he admitted, looking back, "We never became one." A family, that is.

In spite of high hopes and good intentions, they came up against all of the roadblocks to success inherent in a blended family. When asked what the biggest problem was, Neil said, "I didn't know what to do. I felt confused. I couldn't seem to figure out where and how I fit in."

Given the situation, he easily slipped into victim thinking. Admittedly, he asked IQs such as "Why won't the boys accept me?," "When will my wife support my efforts to make this work?," and "Why can't I discipline the children, too?"

Sadly, seven years later, the marriage ended. With the hindsight of his own experience, Neil shared wisdom for stepparents everywhere. He said the most critical goal for a couple coming together is to agree on a "plan for integration." It sounded like a strategy that one would use for business mergers, but he went on to explain, "Unless the couple is in agreement on how it's all going to work, then it won't work."

With little collaboration between Neil and his wife—and no agreed-upon way of bringing him into the family—he fell into the trap of blaming her, the ex-husband, and, to a small extent, the boys. Neil felt frustrated and isolated, and with a lack of communication on many levels, they stood little chance of succeeding.

Later, when he came across John's book *QBQ!*, he realized he could have used the advice years earlier. When we asked him how, he stated, "The QBQ totally applies here—I just needed to ask the right questions as a stepdad."

Neil added, "Since personal accountability begins with me, I should have been the one to define my role, engage the boys, and come to agreement with my wife. But it was easy to blame others while feeling sorry for myself. If there's ever a next time, armed with the QBQ, I'll know what to do."

Exploring possible QBQs he might have asked, Neil quickly came up with these:

"How can I define my role?"

"What can I do to earn the kids' trust and respect?"

"How can I improve communication with my new spouse?"

"What can I do to help create a plan for our success?"

Recently, Neil met with his former stepsons for lunch. It was a little awkward, but somewhere in the conversation the older boy—now a man—said, "Neil, I've got to be honest, we weren't very good to you." Neil responded, "That's okay. It was a difficult time for everyone."

Neil said the young man's comment actually brought some peace to him. It helped him process the pain he was still carrying from the past—not because he believed that the adolescent boys had done anything wrong, but simply because he'd been carrying a ton of guilt for years, believing he'd messed it all up.

Blending families is hard work, for sure. And if it doesn't go well, the question should never be who's at fault. Success in this arena, as in any other, is about individuals asking accountable questions—QBQs. Only when each of us invests the time, effort, and energy in changing the only person that we can—ourselves—will we reap the rewards we seek.

# CHAPTER THIRTY-TWO

# The Grandparent Factor

*The best babysitters, of course, are the baby's grandparents.*
*You feel completely comfortable entrusting your*
*baby to them for long periods, which is why most*
*grandparents flee to Florida.*

—DAVE BARRY

When Michael was ten, he was hanging out in our living room while John and Grandpa Miller were chatting. At seventy-six, Jimmy Miller had made the long trip from Ithaca, New York, to Denver for a rare visit. As John told a story to his father, Michael suddenly jumped in and said, "No, Dad, it didn't happen on Friday. It was Saturday." *Uh-oh.*

In the eyes of the man born in 1921 and raised by parents born in the 1890s, Michael had committed an unforgivable sin: He had not only interrupted his father, he had *corrected* him. John, thinking nothing of it because Michael was actually right, continued on with his story, but Grandpa Miller would have none of it. In a stern voice, he scolded Michael for doing what he'd done.

It wasn't easy, but John came to his young son's defense, saying, "Dad, I don't mind. Mike's right."

One moment, two views on parenting. We've always allowed our children to respectfully and within reason do what Michael did. But for Grandpa Miller—parented in a time when children were "seen and not heard"—it was completely inappropriate.

Grandparents. Where do they fit in? How do they fit in? It seems that parents, more than ever, raise their kids with less help and input from *their* parents. This could be because young parents are simply more independent, or it's the result of our mobile society, where fewer grandparents live next door—or in the same house—as their parents once did. Meanwhile, there is more readily available parenting advice—in books, on television, and on the Internet—than ever before. And with many young parents thinking that they don't want to make the same mistakes that they believe their parents made, they aren't going out of their way to seek guidance from their "elders."

**The risk, though, like any pendulum that swings, is letting it swing too far.**

We read a story in a magazine about a first-time mom who went to check on her newborn and found her mother slathering her infant's head with baby oil. Aghast, the daughter shrieked, "Mom, what are you doing!?" to which Grandma responded that this treatment would help the baby's cradle cap clear up more quickly. The new mother's first thought was, *But I'm the mom now!* She wanted to stop her mother but was so sleep-deprived she went back to bed. The short story is this: Grandma turned out to be right; she knew something her daughter didn't.

Nowadays, it's tempting—and possibly just too easy—to turn to the web or social media to seek answers to parenting questions. Young dads and moms look to their peers—who are just finding their own way—to gain parental wisdom. Why is that?

We wrote earlier about the need to reject the common stereotypes of teens. So it is with grandparents. Our advice is to resist any message that says they're irrelevant. Focus not only on the mistakes you believe they made parenting but also on the successes. Be aware of your own fears and uncertainties as a parent. Tamp down potential worry that a grandparent will "take over" or show you up. Never let your ego get in the way of being the best parent you can be.

Sometimes turning to those who've already been there is a great way to go. But sometimes it isn't. And that is the core of the whole grandparent matter: Parents must decide to what extent they value and desire the input of their parents. As Neil showed us, when blending families it's best to have collaboration and communication resulting in a "plan" to succeed. In a perfect world, it would be good to have a plan concerning the how and when of grandparents' involvement.

As parents, it's *our* job to define the role of Grandma or Grandpa. That's the personal accountability piece, which may require a frank and open conversation with them. If, in your opinion, they don't have good ideas to offer or are not able to help you raise your child, don't ask an IQ like "Why is Mother so pushy?" and "When will my father just stay out of it?" Ask QBQs such as "How can I communicate my expectations?" and "What can I do to set healthy boundaries?"

But also, don't forget this one: "What can I do to learn from someone who has gone before me?" Sometimes, our egos get in our way of learning from those who have much to offer.

And a few tips for grandparents: Be sensitive. Be relevant. Be open to new parenting ways. Know your own child's desires. Seek permission to give advice—and give it sparingly. You certainly have value to add, but remember to respect your child.

When parents and grandparents adapt, communicate, and collaborate, it can be a beautiful time of life for all.

# CHAPTER THIRTY-THREE

# The Financial Piece

*Money won't make you happy . . . but everybody wants
to find out for themselves.*

—ZIG ZIGLAR

Have you ever heard questions like these in your home?

"Why don't I get a bigger allowance?"
"When are you going to get me a cell phone?"
"Why do I have to do chores?"

Or how about this one?

"Why can't I get the newest _____?" (Fill
in the blank!)

As parents, we touch every area of our children's lives.
We affect them physically, spiritually, emotionally, and
mentally—and it's easy to see our responsibility in caring for
them in each of these realms. But what about the financial

piece? What is our accountability for sound teachings around money?

Simply put, it all begins with us. Our first job is to get our *own* financial situation in order—and we know that's not easy.

After we married in 1980, no matter what we earned we had one really bad habit: spontaneous, impulsive, and unnecessary spending. We were never broke nor deeply in debt, but we certainly weren't on solid financial footing—or saving for the future. But around our eighth wedding anniversary—before credit cards had become ubiquitous and debit cards existed—we got our act together.

Here's what happened: We went to a cash-only system. Real money, kept in envelopes. And we began keeping a record of *everything* we spent. We thought about, talked about, and watched over our money. As Dave Ramsey, personal finance author and radio host, says, we "bothered to bother." We cared enough to stay on top of our dollars, knowing where they came from and where they went. It became a purposeful pursuit and practice, and an integral part of our lifestyle.

It wasn't easy fighting those desires of wanting whatever we wanted whenever we wanted it. There was marital stress, too. It was rarely a bonding moment when one of us would ask the other, "Okay, how much did you spend today?"

But, the hassle of monitoring our money was *far less* painful than having the financial wolf at our door. There were many positive outcomes from this exercise, from increasing charitable giving and savings to peace of mind and opportunities to model effective money management for our kids.

Remember the old but powerful phrase "Practice what you preach"? Isn't it a tad hypocritical for parents who've done a less-than-stellar job with their finances to admonish their children to handle their dollars better? We have little right to ask IQs of them like "Why did you spend all your allowance on candy?" or "When will you be more responsible with your money?" until *we* are working on the financial piece, too. Children will make poor choices with their money—it's to be expected. Our job is to be there to coach them through their mistakes, while setting the best example possible ourselves.

Now, when it comes to specific practices, many parents are looking for a magical step-by-step formula for teaching money management skills to their children. Some wonder if it's best to use allowances, budgets, or commissions. "Should we use chore charts with stickers for our young child or give them cash?" they ask. Here's our answer to all parents looking for someone to give them the how-to of parenting: *If it works for your family, then it's a good approach.* There is no "right" way. The key, though, is to first know what lessons we want to instill in our children related to money. Once those lessons are defined, parents can acquire practical how-to's to communicate them by talking to other parents, reading books, attending a class—and sometimes simply trying new things to see what works.

But it all begins with deciding what it is we want to teach. We identified many simple but important lessons to pass on to the Miller kids and would like to share a few here:

- Spend less than you make, it's simple math.
- When it's gone, it's gone.
- Be in debt to no one, short of owning a home.
- Give first to those less fortunate, second to your savings account.
- You don't have to have what others have.
- A used automobile will do the job.
- Decline those offers for credit, even at your favorite store.
- Money comes through working and we were created to work.
- Give 110 percent on the job and you'll always have a job.
- Nothing is deserved—everything is earned.

Lessons like these lay a solid foundation of personal accountability for our kids. But before a parent attempts to teach them, it's important to ask financially responsible QBQs such as:

"How can I identify the traps I fall into and learn
ways to avoid them?"
"What can I do to acquire new financial management skills?"
"How can I best teach my child to handle money
well?"
"What can I do to define the lessons I want my
child to learn?"

By asking these powerful questions and addressing the financial piece of parenting, we will serve ourselves and our children well. And since money is an integral part of our world and always will be, the lessons conveyed to them will prove useful for a lifetime.

# CHAPTER THIRTY-FOUR

# Equipping for Life

*We may not be able to prepare the future for
our children, but we can at least prepare our
children for the future.*

—FRANKLIN D. ROOSEVELT

The twenty-year-old picked up his car from the repair
shop and paid the bill himself. Later that day, he hesitated to
tell his do-it-yourself dad how much the repairs cost. When
he finally shared the amount, his dad was immediately
angry, admonishing his son with "Why didn't you fix your
car yourself?! You could've saved a lot of money!"

The son's first thought: *But you've never shown me how, Dad.*

We know that some people might consider the son's
thought to be victim thinking or blame, but we don't see it
that way. Over the years, we've met late teens and young
adults who seem utterly lost in life. They are good kids but
are floundering. Not only do they appear to have little direc-
tion but they seem to lack the skills and know-how to find
their way. We see all of this as a parental failure.

On many occasions, Karen has asked this rhetorical question:

"Where have all the parents gone?"

We know that might sound a bit judgmental, but the truth is some parents do abdicate their positions as teacher, builder, and guide for their children. Sure, they may have been totally present for the ten-year-old, but somewhere along the way, as the child moves closer to adulthood, the parent is no longer by their side. We're not talking about making the mistake of enabling our child, as we explored in Chapter Twenty; we're talking about dads and moms fulfilling their core parental purpose: equipping children with essential life skills.

There are probably several reasons why parents fail to meet this all-important obligation, everything from not knowing how to do it to being distracted and drained by too many problems of their own. Sometimes, though, parents go off track because they buy into some dangerous and derailing societal messages. Just as we should resist the negative stereotypes about young people, we should also be wary of these messages about parenting:

"You deserve more out of life!"
"Don't lose yourself in your kids!"
"You need lots of 'me' time!"
"Don't let family hold you back!"

Strong, accountable parents resist these messages, as they stay focused on doing everything they are able to do to prep their child for life during the building phase of parenting. They never forget that they made a choice to become a parent and made a commitment to the child. Dads and moms who own the results of their parenting don't ask Incorrect Questions like:

"Why doesn't my son have any common sense?"
"Why aren't you getting your college applications in?"
"When will my daughter show more responsibility?"
"Why can't you manage your money better?"
"When will you get out there and find a job?"
"Why are kids so lazy nowadays?!"

Just as we maintained in Chapter One that young Grayson is a product of his parents' parenting, we suggest to you that if a child isn't equipped to succeed in life, the parents have failed to do their job. So instead of lashing out at their children with IQs or shaming words like "He should know better!" and "I told you so!"—outstanding parents look into that mirror and ask themselves, *Was I there for him? Did I teach her well? What could I have done differently?*

Truly, why would we expect our kids to do life well if we haven't taught them how to do life? Remember, the building phase of parenting is only for a season. When we get to the other side, we surely don't want to find a child who's thinking, *Where did you go, Mom? You put yourself first, Dad. You weren't there for me.*

To make sure that scenario never happens, let's ask a couple QBQs right now: "What can I do to identify and teach the life skills my children will need?" and "How can I best equip them for successful living?"

In the end, when we've been there for our kids, preparing them to have productive and fulfilling lives, we can honestly say that we did life together.

# CHAPTER THIRTY-FIVE

# The Ultimate QBQ

*The only things we can keep are the things we freely
give to God. What we try to keep for ourselves is
just what we are sure to lose.*

—C. S. LEWIS

Outside our Denver home, we have developed a small
habitat for wild birds. It's not unusual to find Karen sneaking
stealthily around the trees trying to catch glimpses of babies
peering out of nests.

One year, we watched as a family of western meadow-
larks grew to a point where there was not enough room in
the nest for them all to fit! While doing her sneaking and
peeking one afternoon, Karen found the little ones perched
on a nearby fence. Every so often they would leave the fence
rail and practice flying by returning to the nest, where they
were nurtured by their parents. This went on for some time,
till one day the babies were nowhere to be found. The chicks
were gone. The nest was empty.

That's what human parenting is all about. One day the
kids are there—and the next day they're not. They've left.

They're independent. A minute ago we were their complete and total authority, and now we watch out the window for them to return—all grown up—with their own kids in tow. That's the way it's supposed to be.

But this normal and healthy process will never happen if the parent doesn't grow, too. Parenting the QBQ way means anticipating, accepting, and adapting to the changing and evolving role of being a dad or mom. Here's a critical concept:

**Parenting never really ends. It changes.**

The things we do for a ten-year-old—nurturing, correcting, protecting—are primarily about *building* that little person into a big person, an adult. Ever so gradually, we are teaching them how to fly, to eventually leave the nest. But then one day the job isn't about building anymore, it's about *relating*. That doesn't mean they can't still learn from us, it's just that as parents *we* must adapt to this new relationship and our new role.

Some parents never get there. They don't adapt. They're stuck. And sadly for all involved, not seeing the need to alter their parenting practices or not knowing how, they attempt to control their adult children, running (ruining?) their kids' lives, constantly nagging and telling them what to do, offering unsolicited and often unwelcome advice. The result?

Frustration mounts, conversations dry up, and relationships falter.

It's not a pretty sight.

But a QBQ parent grows right along with the child, shifting from being the parent who builds to becoming the parent who relates by asking accountable questions like "How can I adapt to my changing world?"—and what we call *The Ultimate QBQ*:

**"How can I let go of what I can't control?"**

These are powerful questions that strong, accountable dads and moms ask to help them evolve in their parenting job. Someone once said that the quietest sound in the world is the sound of letting go. We believe it and, like you, know it's not the easiest thing to do. But it sure does make for good parenting.

# Chapter Thirty-six

# Teaching the QBQ

*Tell me and I forget, teach me and I may remember,*
*involve me and I learn.*

—BENJAMIN FRANKLIN

Can you imagine young people asking any of these IQs?

"Why doesn't anyone understand me?"
"When will my teacher give me a break?"
"Why is school so boring?"
"Who's going to pay for me to attend college?"
"Why don't I have more friends?"
"Who will give me a job?"
"Why do my parents nag me all the time?"
"When will I get what I deserve?"
"Why don't my mom and dad listen to me?"

Obviously, these questions can lead any of us—regardless of age—to play victim, complain, procrastinate, and blame.

And that's why it is important to pass the QBQ on to our kids.

Parents often ask, "Can the QBQ be taught to children?" The answer is yes, and here's how:

We recommend giving your high-school and young-adult offspring the *QBQ!* book to read as they will be able to enjoy the stories, comprehend the content, and put the QBQ to work in their life. For middle schoolers, we suggest parents read the *QBQ!* book *with* them. Rob, a father of two, says it best:

"The extent to which our twelve-year-old daughter eschews personal accountability at every turn is simply breathtaking. Because of that, we started reading two *QBQ!* chapters with her each week. We cover one on Wednesday night and another on Sunday evening. We quiz her on the concepts and how she can use them. This process has provided the structure needed to have good conversation. We're proud to say that she's smart as a whip *and* pleased to report that she's 'getting it'!"

With younger kids, any parent who believes in the QBQ can find opportunities to teach the QBQ. Sometimes it's only in our modeling, but sometimes it's both modeling and instruction on what the QBQ is, why it's important, and how to ask a better question. And it's never too early to start. One dad, though, writes: "I want my children to be accountable

for their actions. I want to instill in them a sense of responsibility. I just don't want them to grow up too fast!" We don't
see a conflict at all. In fact, teaching a young child QBQ *now*
will help them grow up *better*. Let's see how some parents are
teaching personal accountability and the QBQ to their little
ones.

Sheila, a mother of two, writes:

I have noticed my six-year-old daughter, McKennah,
places blame on everyone around her. After studying
*QBQ!* at work, I decided to try to teach her personal
accountability. One afternoon, a wonderful teachable
moment came along.

We were coming out of a store and I was a bit ahead
of McKennah struggling with my own bags. As we
walked, she was messing with a new notebook that had
loose pages and she dropped it in the middle of the
parking lot! She yelled to me, "Mom, you made me
drop my book!" I replied, "How did I make you drop
your notebook?" She said, "You were walking too
fast!"

Once in the car I told her we all make choices and
when things don't go right we have to ask ourselves
what we could have done differently. I gave her an
example by saying, "Here's a question Mommy can ask:
"What more could I have done to help McKennah cross

the parking lot?" She quickly declared, "You could have walked slower!" Biting my tongue, I went on to admit that I could have slowed down or carried the notebook for her. "Now," I said, "it's McKennah's turn!" Referencing the QBQ guidelines, I told her to ask a question starting with "What" or "How" and containing the word "I." After several attempts she came up with "What could I have done to get to the car without dropping my stuff?" Once she got there we were able to talk about solutions such as asking Mommy for help, not looking at the notebook until we got to the car, or asking for a bag to carry it in.

We've learned that even a child can understand and practice asking the right questions!

Sheila clearly shows us that personal accountability can be taught to children. It's also "caught" by kids when they see Mom and Dad practicing it. We must never forget that modeling is the most powerful of all teachers. Sheila parented the QBQ way by modeling QBQ herself and coaching her daughter to apply it in her life. Outstanding!

Anthony, the father of two, shares how making QBQ fun can be a winning strategy:

While driving down the highway on a family road trip, we were talking about school when our first-grade daughter, Coral, said, "My teacher is so unfair. She gave me a yellow light and I didn't even do anything! Why did she do that?" Hearing her ask an Incorrect Question, my wife, Brenda, and I saw an opportunity to teach our kids about the QBQ, so we made up a game. After telling them what a QBQ sounds like, I would ask, "Is it a QBQ to ask, 'Why did my teacher give me a yellow light?' " and they'd respond, "Nooooooooooo!" I would say, "The QBQ is, 'What can I do to get a green light in class?' " Then Brenda would ask another question and the kids would tell us if it was a QBQ or not. It was lots of fun.

A few days later when I was complaining to my wife about something that happened at work, I exclaimed, "Why?! Why do they do that?" From across the kitchen came a sweet correction from Coral, "That's not a QBQ, Daddy!" I was floored, and we began to play the game again. That evening I read the kids a story about a porcupine that had an apple stuck to his back, making him too big to fit into his nest. The porcupine said, "It's not fair! I'll never get into my nest." Although that wasn't technically an IQ, I thought it would be fun to ask the kids what would be the QBQ for our porcupine friend. Coral replied, "What can I do to get all of this stuff off of my back so I can get into my home?" Yes! A flawless QBQ!

The beauty of the QBQ is in its simplicity—and it's never too early to start teaching it to our children. Our lives have been made better by practicing The Question Behind the Question in our home.

P.S.: Whenever it's Coral's younger brother Kenneth's turn to ask a QBQ, his question is always the same: "Can I play with my toys now, please?" Oh well, he'll get it soon.

By making QBQ fun, Anthony and Brenda have done a stellar job passing the QBQ on to their children. As in any building process, a solid base is critical, and what better foundation to give kids to stand on than that of *personal accountability*.

And here's a quick test to see if your child is beginning to think and act accountably. We call it the "spilled milk" metaphor. When the milk glass is lying on its side and its former contents are flowing down the table legs to the floor, does the child say, "The milk spilled!" or "*I* spilled the milk"? Clearly, one statement is personal accountability with a No Excuses underpinning—and the other isn't. As you work to teach your kids the QBQ, listen to their language as it'll tell you a lot about where they are when it comes to absorbing and practicing the message of personal accountability.

So go ahead, teach your kids how to ask QBQs, while also asking them yourself, and see the difference personal accountability makes for the whole family. Remember, the better question—*The Question Behind the Question*—always begins with "What" or "How," contains an "I," and focuses on action.

# CHAPTER THIRTY-SEVEN

# Adopting the QBQ

*One of the greatest diseases is to be nobody to anybody.*
—MOTHER TERESA

For some moms and dads, parenting seems to come easily and they experience mostly smooth sailing. For others, parenting is challenging and it can be a rocky road.

We can relate to both.

As we already shared, our youngest three children are adopted. We had our biological kids—Kristin, Tara, Michael, and Molly—and were done. Or so we thought. Then one day, Charlene, Jazzy, and Natasha, ages five, three, and one, came into our lives and everything changed forever.

Can you say "shell-shocked"?

We'd love to say it was easy in those early days and that "love conquered all," but as we found out, that's often not the case with adoptions. There have been highs and lows, joys and sorrows, good and bad. Speaking as forthrightly and accountably as we can, it wasn't about the three girls—it was all about John and Karen falling into the trap of asking IQs like:

"Why is this happening to us?"
"When is someone going to give us more help and
    support?"
"Whose idea was this anyway?"
"Why didn't the social workers provide us with
    more training?"
"Who exactly said this was going to be easy?"

These questions—asked while under pressure, experiencing change, and living with a new level of fatigue and self-doubt—clearly harmed our ability to parent in an effective way. Looking back, we were caught off-guard by the reality that while remaining true to what we believed to be good parenting, we needed to learn new and different ways to parent these precious girls.

And it all began by parenting the QBQ way:

"How can I learn new parenting practices?"
"What can I do to support my spouse?"
"How can I own the development of these
    girls?"
"What can I do to adapt to my changed world?"

And, of course, *The Ultimate QBQ*: "How can I let go of what I can't control?"

As we've shared throughout this book, the answers are in the questions. Said differently, when we ask better questions, we get better answers. Only when we—John and Karen—began asking QBQs did we achieve the parenting results we sought. More than a decade later, we're a family, we're a team. Perfect? No, not even close. But much further along than if we'd continued to ask lousy questions that led us to victim thinking, complaining, procrastination, and blame. Taking the high road of *personal accountability* helps every mom and dad in that critical role—that chosen role—of building little ones into adults.

# CHAPTER THIRTY-EIGHT

# Practicing the QBQ

*I am still learning.*
—MICHELANGELO

As adults, people often attend a class or training session, listen to a podcast, or finish a book and exclaim, "Wow, I learned a lot!" Well, maybe they did, and maybe they didn't. The truth is, it's challenging to grasp what "learning" really means, so allow us to share three words on this matter:

**Learning equals change.**

If, after attending a seminar or studying a book, our thinking, emotions, and behaviors do not change, how can we claim that we learned anything? Our educational system is frequently based on acquiring knowledge we may never use, but in the day-to-day world of parenting, we need more. We need change. We need action. We need to apply what we've heard or read so we can be the best parents we can be!

With that in mind, let's engage in some much-needed content review because, as we like to say, "Repetition is the motor of learning!" Not only do we encourage you to keep *Parenting the QBQ Way* handy and reread it many times, we especially recommend you frequently return to this particular chapter. Only through many exposures to ideas and methods do they become part of our daily parenting journey as we strive toward raising great kids.

So, here we go!

### A Dozen Key *Parenting the QBQ Way* Principles

The answers are in the questions.
My child is a product of my parenting.
Parenting is a learned skill.
The best parents are no-excuses parents.
Modeling is the most powerful of all teachers.
Outstanding parents do the hard stuff.
Action now is almost always better than later.
Humility is the cornerstone of leadership.
Stress is a choice.
Trust must be earned.
Parenting never really ends. It changes.
I can only change me.

**What to Avoid**

Asking Incorrect Questions (IQs). IQs begin with
  "Why," "When," and "Who."
"Why?" questions lead to victim thinking and com-
  plaining.
"When?" questions lead to procrastination.
"Who?" questions lead to blame and finger-pointing.

**What to Do**

Ask The Question Behind the Question, the QBQ.

**The QBQ Defined**

QBQ is a practical tool that enables parents to
  practice personal accountability by making better
  choices.

**How to Create a QBQ**

1. QBQs begin with the words "What" or "How"—not
   "Why," "When," or "Who."
2. QBQs contain the personal pronoun "I"—not "they,"
   "you," or even "we."
3. QBQs always focus on action.

## TRANSFORMING IQs INTO QBQs

As you review the following examples, which we chose because we hear them time and again, don't get hung up on actual words or content. Remember the purpose of QBQ is to make better choices so we can practice personal accountability. We want to avoid victim thinking, complaining, procrastination, and blame. You can recast any of the following IQs or QBQs to fit your situation:

| IQ | QBQ |
|---|---|
| *Why doesn't my daughter ever take my advice?* | What can I do to get to know her better? |
| *When will my son open up to me?* | How can I build a more trusting relationship? |
| *Who made the mess in here?* | What can I do to help my child learn good habits? |
| *Who will save me from these kids?!* | How can I find joy in being with my children? |
| *Why won't my children obey me?* | What can I do to set clear expectations and consequences—and follow through? |
| *Why aren't teachers more supportive?* | What can I do to support the teacher? |

| IQ | QBQ |
|---|---|
| *Why isn't my son more responsible?* | How can I model responsibility in all I do? |
| *Why is parenting so hard?* | What can I do to learn new skills? |
| *Why isn't my child a better student?* | How can I better understand my child's struggles? |
| *Why doesn't my spouse help me out more?* | How can I better communicate my needs? |
| *Why can't you hang out with different kids?* | How can I get to know my child's friends? |
| *When will my kids start doing what I ask?* | What can I do to confront lovingly yet firmly? |
| *Why does my child challenge me so?* | How can I draw clear, loving lines in the sand? |
| *Who is going to take care of this problem?* | How can I propose a solution? |
| *Why does my child seem to lack drive and ambition?* | What can I do teach the value of work? |
| *Why is my toddler so difficult?* | How can I acquire strong parenting practices? |
| *When will he change?* | What can I do to change me? |
| *Who's going to help my child get better grades?* | What can I do to help my child? |

| IQ | QBQ |
|---|---|
| *When are you going to manage your time better?* | How can I provide the tools my child needs? |
| *Why won't my kids listen?* | How can I improve my listening skills? |
| *When will they do what I ask?* | What can I do to follow through? |
| *Why don't my kids study harder?* | How can I demonstrate a solid work ethic? |
| *Why is my son so moody?* | How can I understand what's driving his emotions? |
| *When will my daughter be more respectful?* | What can I do to show her respect? |
| *Why do my kids want so much?* | How can I show contentment in my life? |
| *Why don't you do what I tell you?* | What can I do right now to know what's happening in your world? |
| *When will young people stop expecting everything to be handed to them?* | What can I do to identify and eliminate my own entitlement thinking? |
| *Why does he whine about everything I ask him to do?* | How can I lovingly, firmly confront this behavior? |

| IQ | QBQ |
|---|---|
| *Why are my kids so frustrating?* | How can I show my children that I love them just as they are? |
| *Why is my child so rebellious?!* | What can I do right now to control my emotions? |
| *When will she stop dressing like that?* | How can I establish better standards? |
| *When will he stop doing that?* | What can I do to lift my child up today? |
| *When will my spouse support me more?* | How can I be as supportive as possible? |
| *Who tracked mud in all over the hallway floor?* | What can I do right now to deal with this calmly? |
| *Why do my kids manage their money so poorly?* | How can I set a good example for them? |
| *Why is my teen so distant?* | How can I better connect with him? |
| *When will my kid stop complaining so much?* | What can I do to be more positive? |
| *Why are people so critical?* | What can I do to find the good? |

| IQ | QBQ |
|---|---|
| *When will he stop ruling this house with his tantrums?* | How can I apply the "Discipline D's"? (pages 57–58) |
| *When will my kids stop bickering?* | What can I do to teach them how to work through their differences? |

And remember, when you just don't know what else to do or what QBQ to ask, there's always *The Ultimate QBQ*:

"How can I let go of what I can't control?"

"The Question Behind the Question" has made all the difference in our world, and it's our hope that it will in your world as well. But like any tool, it is of no value unless it's used. So pick it up, carry it with you—and put it to work every day. We know by parenting the QBQ way, you will be the outstanding mom or dad you wish to be, and your kids will thank you for it—someday.

And finally, let's state the not so obvious: The need for personal accountability never ends. So, it's always the right time to use the QBQ. One woman wrote, "My teenage son is struggling so much right now, I'm afraid if I start using your recommendations and bring more personal accountability into our home, he might not graduate from high school."

In other words, she feared doing the right things—the *tough* things—right now. We responded simply: "It's never too late to start being a strong, accountable parent."

We hope you agree. Please share your parenting stories with us at John@QBQ.com or Karen@QBQ.com. We'd love to hear from you!

# Getting More Out of QBQ!

QBQ Inc. offers several valuable products and services. Please visit QBQ.com to learn about:

- Securing a member of the QBQ Inc. team to speak at your organization, conference, or event.
- *QBQ! The Question Behind the Question.* The bestselling book that started it all!
- *Flipping the Switch*, the companion book to *QBQ!* that takes the QBQ to the next level.
- *Outstanding! 47 Ways to Make Your Organization Exceptional*, the book that enables organizations to excel.
- *I Own It! Building Character Through Personal Accountability.* A curriculum focused on personal accountability for teachers' use in the classroom.

- *Specks & Planks,* a practical study enabling individuals, couples, small groups, and churches to connect *QBQ!* and *Flipping the Switch* to the Bible.
- The easy-to-implement, multimedia training system *Personal Accountability and the QBQ!* designed to be implemented in-house by an organization's internal facilitators.
- *QBQ! QuickNotes.* Subscribe to stories of personal accountability and outstanding service at our sites.

**QBQ Inc.**
**Helping Organizations Make Personal**
**Accountability a Core Value®**
**email: info@QBQ.com**
**QBQ.com**
**OutstandingOrganization.com**

# · About the Authors ·

Daughter Tasha Cardenas, son-in-law Ricardo Cardenas, daughter Molly, daughter Kristin Lindeen, son-in-law Erik Lindeen, daughter Jazzy, son Michael, grandson Joshua Lindeen, John Miller, daughter Charlene, Karen Miller, daughter Tara Gallagher, son-in-law Justin Gallagher.

**John G. Miller,** a Cornell University graduate and founder of QBQ Inc., has been involved in the training and development industry since 1986. He has worked with hundreds of Fortune 500 companies and government and nongovernment organizations and thousands of individuals to help them make personal accountability a core value. Miller, who has appeared on national television and radio, is the author of *QBQ! The Question Behind the Question, Flipping the Switch: Unleash the Power of Personal Accountability Using the QBQ!*, and *Outstanding! 47 Ways to Make Your Organization Exceptional.*

**Karen G. Miller** has served as a mentor to other moms in MOPs (Mothers of Preschoolers) and MomsNext. She has held leadership positions in Bible Study Fellowship. Karen was a registered nurse for sixteen years.

John and Karen Miller live in Denver, Colorado, and have been married since 1980. They have seven children.

# Helping businesses, organizations, and families make personal accountability a core value.

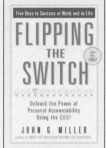

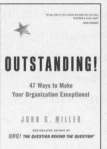

**QBQ!**
ISBN 978-0-399-15233-7

**Flipping the Switch**
ISBN 978-0-399-15295-5

**Outstanding!**
ISBN 978-0-399-15640-3

**Parenting the QBQ Way**
ISBN 978-0-399-16192-6